PACKHORSE, WAGGON AND POST

STUDIES IN SOCIAL HISTORY

edited by

HAROLD PERKIN

Senior Lecturer in Social History, University of Lancaster

THE OUTLAWS OF MEDIEVAL LEGEND — Maurice Keen

RELIGIOUS TOLERATION IN ENGLAND, 1787–1833 — Ursula Henriques

LEARNING AND LIVING, 1790–1960: A Study in the History of the English Adult Education Movement — J. F. C. Harrison

HEAVENS BELOW: Utopian Experiments in England, 1560–1960 — W. H. G. Armytage

FROM CHARITY TO SOCIAL WORK in England and the United States — Kathleen Woodroofe

ENGLISH LANDED SOCIETY in the Eighteenth Century — G. E. Mingay

ENGLISH LANDED SOCIETY in the Nineteenth Century — F. M. L. Thompson

A SOCIAL HISTORY OF THE FRENCH REVOLUTION — Norman Hampson

CHURCHES AND THE WORKING CLASSES IN VICTORIAN ENGLAND — K. S. Inglis

A SOCIAL HISTORY OF ENGLISH MUSIC — E. D. Mackerness

THE PROFESSION OF ENGLISH LETTERS — J. W. Saunders

EDUCATION IN RENAISSANCE ENGLAND — Kenneth Charlton

A HISTORY OF SHOPPING — Dorothy Davis

THE RISE OF THE TECHNOCRATS: A Social History — W. H. G. Armytage

ANCIENT CRETE: A Social History from Early Times until the Roman Occupation — R. F. Willetts

PACKHORSE, WAGGON AND POST: Land Carriage and Communications under the Tudors and Stuarts — J. Crofts

PACKHORSE, WAGGON AND POST

Land Carriage and Communications under the Tudors and Stuarts

by

J. Crofts

LONDON: Routledge and Kegan Paul
TORONTO: University of Toronto Press

First published 1967
in Great Britain by
Routledge and Kegan Paul Limited
and in Canada by
University of Toronto Press

Printed in Great Britain by
W. & J. Mackay & Co. Ltd., Chatham

SBN 7100 4566 2

For Ann

Contents

Illustrations

Between pages 132 and 133

Preface

THIS book traces the development of land communications in England under the Tudors and Stuarts, and illustrates its influence on social life. It deals with the roads, the types of transport, the work of packmen and waggoners, the use of footposts, the establishment of rapid hackney stages, the posting system, the Royal Posts and their privileges, and ends with a note on the early stage coaches. I am indebted for much kind help over the illustrations to the staff of the following: the Controller of H.M. Stationery Office, the Department of Prints and Drawings in the British Museum, the Department of Printed Books in the Bodleian Library, the Curator and Librarian of the Bruce Castle Museum in the Borough of Haringey.

ABBREVIATIONS USED IN THE NOTES

Articles 1584	See under Orders.
C.B.P.	Calendar of Border Papers.
C.P.R.	Calendar of Patent Rolls.
C.S.P. Dom.	Calendar of State Papers (Domestic).
Dasent	Acts of the Privy Council, edited by J. R. Dasent.
H.M. Com.	Reports of the Historical Manuscripts Commission.
Hyde	The Early History of the Post in Grant and Farm, by J. Wilson Hyde, 1894.
Jackman	The Development of Transportation in Modern England, by W. J. Jackman, 1916.
L.P.F.D.	Letters and Papers Foreign and Domestic.
Ordinances 1557	Ordinances for the Postes and Hackneymen bitwene London and Dover. S.P. 12. XLI, 72. Described as 'set forth by Q. Marie'.
Orders 1575	'Orders appointed by the Queens most excellent Majesty'. Described in Stowe MS. 570 as 'Orders devised for the Postes but not passed'.
Orders 1583	Orders appointed by the Lords. Lansdowne MS. LXXVIII, 93. Misdated 1590. Earlier than 1584. Corrections in Burghley's hand.

Orders and Articles printed in 1584, 1603, 1609 etc.

P.O. Accounts	Declared Accounts (Pipe) of the Master of the Posts.
R.C.P. Scotland	Register of the Privy Council of Scotland.
Sadler	State Papers and Letters of Sir Ralph Sadler, edited by Clifford, 1809.
S.P. 12, 14, 16 etc.	State Papers of Elizabeth, James I and Charles I (Domestic Series) as indexed in the Record Office.

I

Packhorse and Waggon

WHEN a load of coals was brought in a cart from East Kilbride to Cambuslang (near Glasgow) in 1723 'crowds of people went out to see the wonderful machine; they looked with surprise and returned with astonishment'.[1]

Such a scene of excitement could hardly have occurred in southern England at any date since the Norman Conquest. Under the manorial system 'Carrying services' by cart or wain were common, and by the time of the Tudors the Court, when on progress, was able to rely upon '400 carewares' requisitioned 'out of the countries adjoining'; whereby, says Harrison, 'the ancient use of somers and sumpter horses is in a manner utterly relinquished, which causeth the trains of our Princes in their progresses to shew far less than those of the Kings of other nations'.[2]

But although a 'strong axle treed cart that is clouted and shod' had become standard farm equipment in Tusser's East Anglia, it was not such a common possession elsewhere. In 1607 the parish of Weybridge, for instance, begs to be excused from supplying transport for the Queen's journey to Oatlands on the ground that they have 'but one cart in the parish',[3] and in many parts of Tudor and Stuart England wheeled vehicles were hardly

[1] H. Graham. *The Social Life of Scotland in the Eighteenth Century*, 1906, p. 167.
[2] *A Description of England*, 1577, Bk. III, 8.
[3] Petition quoted in *Archaeologia*, Vol. VIII, p. 239.

used at all. A traveller of 1637 found Cornwall entirely destitute of 'ought that is moved upon wheels. All carriage is layde upon horses backs, either in trusses or on crookes, or in panniers or peds, which they call pots'.[1]

Most of Devonshire was in the same condition. Although Plymouth was an important naval base, Raleigh reported in 1593 that ordnance could not be conveyed thither by land: 'the passages will not give leave'.[2] The roads could be described as 'mere gullies, worn by torrents in the rocks, which appeared in steps as stair cases with fragments lying loose in the indentures'. Celia Fiennes describes a special kind of narrow waggon which was used in 'the opener wayes' on the eastern border of the county, and this type of vehicle may have been the 'hock cart' of Herrick's poem; but almost all farm work was done by packhorse. Even a century later, when many of the roads had been made fit for wheels, the old methods persisted. 'I have seen building stone', says the agriculturist W. Marshall in 1796, 'carried on horseback along the finest road in the Kingdom, close by the side of which they were raised, and conveyed to a neighbouring town through which the road passed'.[3]

Similar conditions prevailed in Northumberland—('not a cart in the country', says a traveller of 1749)[4]—and, as one might expect, in the Lake District. Celia Fiennes found Kendal full of pack-horses, and the only carts that she saw in use about Windermere were small tumbrils with wheels fixed to a revolving axle. 'The reason is plaine', she says, 'from the narrowness of the Lanes: where is good lands they will lose as little as they can, and where it's hilly and stoney no other Carriages can pass'.[5]

When Sir Daniel Fleming of Rydal tries to arrange for a carrier between Kendal and Whitehaven in 1685, there is no talk of waggons. 'The Kendal carriers bring their packs into Kendal about noon every Wednesday', he writes, 'and set forward for London the Munday following'. He thinks it will be impossible to find a man who will do the journey to Whitehaven and back between Wednesday and Monday; but if between

[1] *A Journey into the West of England*, 1637, Harleian MS. 6494.

[2] Worth. *A History of Plymouth*, 1890, p. 335.

[3] W. Marshall. *Rural Economy of the West of England*, 1796. I, 294.

[4] Quoted by Jackman, p. 142.

[5] *Through England on a side saddle* (The diary of Celia Fiennes, ed. Griffiths, 1888), p. 160.

Wednesday and the following Monday week would be good enough he would recommend 'Charles Udal of this town, who hath a good set of horses (with bells &c)'.[1] This was of course exceptionally hilly and difficult country, but packhorse traffic was the rule also in Lancashire, Yorkshire, Derbyshire, Shropshire and Staffordshire. Until 1760 there was no road for wheeled traffic from Liverpool to Manchester, and the best that the local carrier could offer for the conveyance of invalids or expectant mothers was an easy pad nag.[2] In 1689 a runaway prentice boy, desperately ill, was brought back on a horse from Dewsbury to Huddersfield through bitter March hail storms, arriving collapsed and dead in the saddle, and with the side of his face beaten to pulp on the saddle bow. Although he had received some kindness and attention from compassionate villagers on the road, nobody seems to have thought of putting him in a cart. If carts existed in that bleak country side, they had presumably been laid up for the winter, and were not to be turned out for runaway prentice boys.[3]

In 1718 the Derbyshire justices consider the dangerous condition of Alport ford, on the road between Derby and Stockport. 'Carriers with loaden horses and passengers cannot pass the said ford without great danger of being cast away'. They decide that a horse bridge is urgently needed for the 'great gangs of London Carriers' horses, as well as great drifts of Malt Horses and other daily carriers and passengers'.[4] There is no word of a bridge for wheeled traffic, evidently because the need of it was not felt. Until at least the middle of the eighteenth century all goods sent from Derby or Nottingham to Manchester or to London, all the Yorkshire clothing products, and all the Manchester and Coventry wares were transported on horseback, 'not to London only', says Defoe, 'but to all parts of England, . . . the Manchester men being, saving their wealth, a kind of Pedlars, who carry their goods themselves to the country shop keepers everywhere, as do now the Yorkshire and Coventry manufacturers also'.[5]

This does not mean that in these northern districts wheeled

[1] M. L. Armitt. *Rydal*, 1916, p. 453.
[2] Quoted by Jackman, p. 147.
[3] *Depositions from York Castle* (Surtees Soc., 1861), item cclxii.
[4] J. Cox. *Three Centuries of Derbyshire Annals*.
[5] *The Complete English Tradesman*, 1725, Ch. XXVI.

traffic might not sometimes be used in an emergency. From time to time Lord Howard of Naworth had heavy goods conveyed from London to Newcastle by sea, thence to Newburn by wherry, and from there to Naworth by waggon along 'that hideous road along the Tyne' which in 1680 was still' for the so many and sharp Turnings and perpetual precipices, for a Coach (not sustained by main Force) impassable'.[1]

Similar haulage, *via* Barnard Castle and Stainmore, was undertaken by the German miners who worked the Keswick copper mines from 1569 onwards; and on one occasion when their director, Daniel Hochstetter, brought his wife and five children over from Germany in 1571, the party actually travelled the whole way to Keswick in a vehicle, especially equipped with cushions and with 'chains to stretch under it' by the carrier, at a cost of £10.

But these were really minor feats of engineering, too expensive for ordinary use. When Hochstetter and his wife rode on horseback from London to Keswick the carrier's charges were only £2 *6s. 8d.*, and the same contrast is to be seen in the freight charges for goods. Dutch chairs, warming pans, groceries, thin oven sheeting—anything that could be carried on a horse's back—came all the way from London to Keswick at a penny a pound. But when heavy machinery or casks of wine had to be carted from Newcastle over Stainmore (less than half the distance) the cost worked out at about fourpence a pound, exclusive of tolls and other incidental expenses.[2] Theoretically waggon traffic should have been cheaper, because a horse can draw a much heavier load than it can carry. But only over a good road: not over Stainmore in Elizabeth's time. Until the roads could be made fit for wheels packhorse traffic was actually less costly. In 1584 Sir Ralph Sadler points out that various household things required for the Queen of Scots at Tutbury 'maye be brought downe on horsback by the caryers of Derby and of this town for less than 1d a *lib*. And so may the plate be also brought in a tronk, well malid in canvas, much better chepe than by cart'.[3] As soon as the Turnpike Acts had begun to make some of the roads

[1] *The Household Books &c of Lord William Howard of Naworth* (Surtees Soc., 1874); Roger North, *The Life of Francis North Baron of Guilford*, 1742, p. 139.

[2] Accounts of the Augsburg company printed in W. Collinwood's *Elizabethan Keswick*, 1912. (Cumberland and Westmoreland Antiquarian Soc., Tract 8.)

[3] Sadler III, 261.

fit for wheels the rate for carriage by pack was fixed by the justices at so much a hundredweight higher than the rate for carriage by waggon; but even then the packhorse was found cheaper for some purposes because it moved very much faster. There were, indeed, some exceptions to this. The heavy malt horses from Essex which plodded solemnly into London in the early morning, with the malt men sprawling asleep on the sacks, could be taken by Dekker as an emblem of sloth. But the northern pack trains evidently went at a lively pace. Nashe, speaking of the secret bribes accepted by unjust judges, says that 'by night corrupt gifts and rewards rush in at their gates in whole Armies, like northern carriers coming to their inn'.[1] Especially rapid pack trains seem to have been used, as one might expect, in the fish trade. Defoe says that the Workington men 'carry salmon, fresh as they take them, up to London upon Horses which, changing often, go night and day without intermission, and, as they say, outgo the Post, for that the fish come very sweet and good to London, where the extraordinary price they yield, from 2*s*. 6*d*. to 4*s*. per lb., pays very well for the carriage. They do the same from Carlisle'. This was in the early eighteenth century; but similar fish trains were running from Rye in 1608, from Lyme Regis at about the same date, from Newcastle in 1592, and probably much earlier from other places.[2] Their effect is to be seen in the rapidly falling market for fresh water fish. It is true that in the seventeenth century London fishmongers were still prepared to make a bid for the carp in a gentleman's ponds.[3] But a handsome carp of eighteen inches, which had been worth 4*s*. in the reign of Henry VIII, could command a price of only 1*s*. 4*d*. in 1581. For the carp, which is a bony and bothersome table fish,[4] had owed its great prestige in earlier days largely to the fact that it could be kept alive for days and even weeks in a hamper of wet straw, and could thus be delivered fresh at a great distance by the simplest and slowest form of

[1] Thomas Dekker. *The Seven Deadly Sins of London*, 1608; Thomas Nashe. *Works*, ed. McKerrow, I, 285. See Note 024.

[2] Defoe. *A Tour of Great Britain*, 1724; *H.M. Com.* Report, III, p. 309. S. Webb. *The King's Highway*, p. 77; Dekker. *Lanthorne and Candlelight*, 1608, Ch. VIII.

[3] *Covenants concluded and Made by the Officers of the Greencloth with Robert Parker and George Hill, Yeomen Purveyors of Fresh water Fish*, 1543; *The Losely Manuscripts*, ed. Kemp, 1836, p. 276 (Letter from Henry Sledd). And see Note 01.

[4] See Note 02.

transport. Now the trotting pack-horses were making sea fish more readily available, and in many an ancient fish pond the venerable carp were left to slumber in their medieval mud. Similar fish trains were used by the fish-rippers of Calais and Dieppe, who maintained a rapid service to Paris, and it was made a ground of complaint against the Postmaster for Foreign Parts in 1613 that he had allowed official dispatches to be carried by this means, so that 'it is growen a by word in France that the fishe Rippers of France, who often bring packetts to Diepe, are the King of Englands Messengers'.[1]

There was therefore a good deal to be said for the packhorse even where waggons could have been used, and once accepted as a convenient means of transport it was likely to become permanent for a curious reason. It had been found that in a difficult country of steep hills and boggy valleys the ploughing and heavy hauling was best done by oxen. 'In stiff pulls of every kind, most especially in going up steep hills', writes the agriculturist Marshall in 1796, 'a pair of oxen are considered a sheet anchor. Horses, it is argued, are fearful and soon lost their feet in a slippery road; while oxen, where they are unable to proceed, will always stand their ground. Indeed oxen seem to be considered as essentially necessary in an awkward hilly country.'[2] A very similar opinion was expressed by the Australian 'bullocky' quoted by C. E. Bean:–

> 'In a hole gimme the bullocks. A 'orse is good to go when he's at it, but he hasn't got the heart. If 'orses get fixed for twenty minutes they're punctured. They won't pull any more, however long you stay there. But bullocks—they'll go back nex' day and pull the same as ever.'[3]

As a result of this contrast in animal psychology the ploughing and heavy hauling in the difficult district of the north and west had, from time immemorial, been done chiefly by oxen, and this had had its effect upon the roads. An ox's hoof splays slightly as it is thrust into the mud, and contracts as it is withdrawn, thus enabling the animal to keep going over soft ground in which a horse would soon be bogged. Hence it had been a common

[1] *Petition of Henry Huntley*, S.P. 14, LIV. 51.
[2] W. Marshall. *Rural Economy of Yorkshire*, 1788, I, 263.
[3] C. E. Bean. *On the Wool Track*, 1916, Ch. XX. See Note 03.

practice in these districts to leave the haulage way soft, and make a narrow causeway alongside it for the pack-horses. And once this had been done it was not easy to alter. A causeway was much cheaper and easier to keep in repair than a full width road, and the parish concerned could always plead that it was responsible only for a 'pack and prime way', as it was called: not for a waggon road.[1] Thus a vicious circle was established. They made a causeway because they had left the road soft, and they continued to leave the road soft because they had made a causeway. In this way packhorse traffic tended to perpetuate itself, and these narrow causeways spread everywhere, near York, Skipton, Preston, Wigan, over Blackstone Edge, near Halifax, in Shropshire and Cheshire, as well as in the south-west about Exeter and Ashburton. A company of travellers in 1739 is described as riding the whole way from Glasgow to Grantham on these narrow pack and prime ways.[2]

In the southern and south-eastern counties (except perhaps in Sussex) the traffic presented a different appearance. It is true that here too the packhorse was frequently used, and it is probable that at the beginning of the sixteenth century it was still the chief means of transport. The men who carried for the Pastons in Suffolk, for the Lestranges in Norfolk and for the Stonors in Oxfordshire were all apparently packmen or 'pedders', and so, it may be noted, was the typical carrier as he appears in Elizabethan fiction: 'Derick, Goodman Hobling's man of Kent', who figures in *The famous Victories of Henry V*, and the Rochester carriers in Shakespeare's *Henry IV*. But there can be no doubt that by the middle of the century waggon traffic was well established in these districts, and that it was rapidly increasing.

Stow gives 1564 as the year when 'began long waggons to come in use, such as now com to London from Canterbury, Norwich, Ipswich, Gloucester &c with passengers and commodities',[3] and his rough indication of the area served by these heavy wheeled vehicles can be corroborated from other sources. When the proclamation against the use of four wheeled waggons was issued in 1618, it was the carriers of Sussex, Hampshire, Wiltshire, Berkshire, Oxfordshire and Northamptonshire who

[1] S. Webb. *The King's Highway*, p. 65.
[2] H. Graham. *The Social Life of Scotland*, p. 44.
[3] Stow. *Annales*.

joined in signing a petition against it, and those who were charged at Quarter Sessions with infringing the new regulation all belonged to the same or contiguous counties.[1] In Taylor's *Carrier's Cosmography* 1637 and *A Direction for the English Traveller* 1643 waggons or coaches are noted as coming to London from towns in Essex, Suffolk, Leicestershire, Cambridgeshire, Surrey, Hertfordshire, Northamptonshire, Wiltshire and Gloucestershire.

It would appear therefore that a line drawn across the map from the Wash to Gloucester, and thence curving southward to Weymouth, would include within its arc all the districts where a heavy wheeled traffic was well established in the early seventeenth century; and it may be worth noting that this area corresponds almost exactly with that in which, as N. Gras has shown,[2] corn was cheapest in the fourteenth and fifteenth centuries. One may perhaps guess that it was the problem of marketing a large surplus that had induced the south eastern farmer to set up what, on tolerable roads at least, is the more economical means of transport. In the north and west where crops were comparatively light, and easily disposed of in the local markets, there had perhaps never been the same inducement to set up a wheeled traffic, even where roads would have permitted it, while the greater mobility and adaptability of the packhorse made it far more suitable for dealing with the small consignments and scattered operations of the northern wool and cloth trade.[3]

[1] H.M. Com. (Var. Col., Vol. IV).
[2] N. Gras. *The Evolution of the English Corn Market*, 1915.
[3] H. Heaton. *The Yorkshire Woollen and Worsted Industries*, 1920, p. 200.

II

The Weather

BUT in this rough division of the map into a packhorse area and a waggon area nothing has been said about the weather, and in a country of unmetalled roads this was of primary importance. On the sixteenth-century farm all the heavy hauling of lime or marl for the fields, gravel for the lanes, timber for the fences and 'coals or other necessary fuel fetched far off' had to be done as far as possible in the summer while the roads were still dry and firm. Fitzherbert recommends May for the work, Tusser August, Markham June. Sir Justinian Isham got his coal in in May, Lady Sussex in July; and when, owing to the exceptionally wet summer of 1725 Nicholas Blundell of Crosby failed to get his in, and had to buy coal by the pack load in winter, he notes it as a thing 'never known before'.[1] About the end of October the prudent farmer, like Best of Elmswell near Driffield, laid up his waggon, and sent his corn to market during the winter months on a string of eight pack-horses, tied head to tail, with a couple of men to 'guide the pokes'.[2] Best notes that the first time waggons were seen at Malton market in 1641, the year when he wrote, was on 30 April, and he clearly thought it too early in the season. 'It is ill going to Malton with draughts', he says, 'when the fields adjoining to the highway are most of them fough' (i.e. 'fog'; meaning here, perhaps, the new hay

[1] *Blundell's Diary*. ed. T. E. Gibson, 1895, p. 212.
[2] *The Farming Book of Henry Best, of Elmswell* (Surtees Soc., 33).

grass that must not be trampled). Best was a Yorkshireman, and therefore perhaps prejudiced in favour of pack-horses, but his objection to the use of waggons while the roads were still soft was common sense anywhere. The Hertfordshire maltsters and loaders always carried on horseback between Michaelmas and Mayday 'in former times',[1] says a petition of 1631, and there can be little doubt that all carriers followed the same rule if they possibly could. Sir Ralph Verney writing from London on 27 April 1636 about some heavy goods that he wishes to send down to Claydon, 'would faine have the Carrier (Plaistow of East Claydon) bring up a cart about this day fortnight if it may be no prejudice to him'—implying a doubt whether Plaistow would be willing to use a cart so early in the year.[2]

But during the sixteenth century great changes had taken place in the economic pattern of the country. It has been estimated that in 1500 the population of London was only about 50,000, or 2 per cent of the total population of England: by 1605 it had risen to something like 224,000, or nearly 6 per cent.[3] This alone would be enough to cause great changes in the bulk and direction of traffic in the south-eastern counties. The demand for four or five times the amount of fresh foodstuffs in London made prices soar, and in the remoter parts of Suffolk or Essex many a small farmer, whose father had had to be content with the local market, now found it profitable to send his stuff all the way to Town.

But far more important in its effect upon traffic was the fact that during the same period the general trade of London had increased tenfold, rising from 44 per cent of the whole trade of the country (the estimated figure for 1506) to nearly 80 per cent in 1604. Most of this increase was no doubt maritime, and some of it, trade carried coastwise or by inland waterways. But one cannot doubt that this phenomenal increase had brought a much greater pressure of wheeled traffic upon the roads. Certain trades seem to have been particularly dependent on wheeled transport in wet weather, notably malting. During Elizabeth's reign commercial brewing had developed consider-

[1] See footnote on p. 11.

[2] There was however a plague scare at the time, and carriers may have been forbidden to travel.

[3] N. Gras. *The Evolution of the English Cornmarket*, 1915.

ably in London, where the water was regarded as exceptionally good for the purpose, and London beer was exported in large quantities to Flanders and Hambourg. In 1559 the export was only 328 tuns; by 1590 it had risen to something like 2,000 tuns, and its reputation at home may be judged by the fact that Lord Howard thought it worth his while to have a hogshead sent all the way to Naworth by way of Newcastle and Newburn.

To supply the brewers, there had grown up in Hertfordshire and the eastern counties a brisk malting industry, and a speculative growing and selling of barley which in 1608 gave the Privy Council some concern.[1] It appeared that many farmers had taken to sowing barley instead of wheat, and that in Hertfordshire especially, crowds of 'poor folk of mean ability, widows, servants and the like' were keeping themselves off the parish by buying barley in small quantities, getting it malted, and selling it to the brewers' agents. Now malt needs dry manufacture and dry carriage; if its moisture content rises above 3 per cent it is soon spoilt. But these people were, of course, malting 'at unseasonable tymes of the year', since they had to live all the year round; and in order to get their product to the brewers in good condition during the winter months wheeled transport had to be used. The roads had thus been reduced to a series of sloughs, and in 1631 the Hertfordshire justices complain that between Royston and Buntingford they 'are daily torn up with malt carts, who commonly carry 14 quarters of malt weight at one time. Unless maltsters and loaders be enjoined to carry on horseback between All Saints and May Day, as in former times, there will not be found materials in the country to repair the roads nor make them passable'. An order was made to this effect, and a certain Thomas Archer was summoned for disregarding it. He pleaded that 'he had sent not above 3 or 4 loads through the highways by cart, and further, that he had hired a man to carry his corn on horseback, save only when his own team brought home coals for the supply of his household'.[2] Another trade that seems to have relied chiefly upon wheeled transport was that of the western clothier.

In the north the cloth trade was a cottage industry, and the clothier was not so much a producer as a go between, who

[1] *The Stiffkey Papers* (Camden Soc.), p. 57.
[2] A. Kingston. *A History of Royston*, 1906, p. 132.

bought the raw material and arranged for its distribution among the scattered workers, subsequently collecting and marketing the finished goods. For this kind of activity the packhorse must have been indispensable, and since the bulk of these northern kerseys were exported to Flanders to be dyed and finished, the risk of damage in transit was not perhaps very serious.

But the fine dyed and finished cloths of Wiltshire needed more weatherproof carriage, and the conditions under which they were produced made this easier to arrange. Instead of scattered workers and a middleman organizer we find in these districts the beginnings of a factory system: hundreds of wage workers gathered under one roof, and carrying out the whole process of manufacture from raw material to finished goods with tools and appliances provided by the clothier. Thomas Deloney describes the famous 'Jack of Newbury' (John Winchcomb) as employing 200 men at his looms, more than 100 as shearmen, dyers and fullers, and more than 300 women as carders and spinners; all apparently under the same roof or within the same group of buildings.[1] The figures may be exaggerated, but he is undoubtedly describing a factory technique; and for a trade so organized transport by waggon or cart was obviously most practical and economical. The southern clothier was saved all that sending and fetching in small lots which marked every stage of the northern manufacture, he had merely to load up his waggons in his own yard, and he could probably get his wares to market with far fewer horses than his northern rival was obliged to use. True, his horses were heavy draft animals, more expensive to keep; and the waggons themselves no doubt cost him something considerable in maintenance and repairs. But on tolerable roads there could be no doubt that they were the more economical means of transport; and even if the roads were bad, there was the overriding consideration that waggons were dryer and safer. If a packhorse gets bogged, the first thing to do is to relieve it of its load, and how that is to be done in a swampy place without wetting the contents of its pack may be a difficult problem. But if a waggon gets stuck in a slough, it may indeed require borrowed teams and a great deal of shouting to get it out again; but in the mean time the load will not be damaged

[1] Some account of these factories is given in O. Mann's *Works of Thomas Deloney*, 1912.

if the slush does not rise above the axle trees. The advantages are so obvious that Deloney's picture in *Thomas of Reading* (1600) of the western roads blocked for hours at a time by the passage of clothiers' carts and waggons, though no doubt a romantic exaggeration, may safely be taken as presenting a real feature of contemporary road conditions. The further a traveller went along the western road from Staines 'the more waines and more he met continually'.

It was probably the trades dealing in perishable goods, of which malt and fine cloth may be taken as examples, that first brought a heavy wheeled traffic upon the roads in winter; and once the practice had started, other trades were almost bound to follow suit for purely mechanical reasons.

III

The Roads

THE Tudor governments had made some effort to deal with the problem of the roads, and the system of repair by statue labour under parish overseers, set up by the Acts of 1555 and 1563, worked well enough in remote country places to survive until the nineteenth century. What they had failed and perhaps without the help of Dutch engineers could not have attempted to do, was to establish any standard or prescribe any technique of road-making; and this was a fatal omission.

It is clear from the methods of repair usually adopted that a road was hardly regarded as a structure at all. It was commonly thought of as a strip of land upon which no member of the community had the right to sow his peas, or stack his manure, or dig his marl. It is true that over-thrifty individuals frequently tried to use it in this way; but public opinion was against them for the simple reason that once a highway was blocked the King's lieges had a statutory right to make their way over the land adjoining to their destination.[1] This right was well understood by the public of the seventeenth century, and was exercised so freely as to constitute a serious menace to agriculture. A gentleman like Sergeant Hoskins, contemplating a journey by coach in 1627, would order his servants as a matter of course 'to study the coach-way; where to break hedges, and how to

[1] See C. H. Hartman. *The Story of the Roads*, 1927, p. 46.

avoid deep and dangerous ways';[1] and Justice Ellwood's coachman 'seeing a nearer and easier way than the common road through a cornfield, and that it was wide enough to run without damaging the corn', turned into the cornfield without hesitation.[2] In winter especially, when a highway had become in parts impassable the traffic was compelled to use 'driftways on trespass through the neighbouring enclosures', with the result that the original line of the road was sometimes forgotten and superseded. 'Travellers begge passage through another's grounds in winter' says Thomas Adams in a sermon of 1630, 'for avoydance of the Miry wayes, and so long use it on sufference that at last they plead it by Prescription, and hold it by Custome.' The problem was particularly grievous in the close-farming districts of the south east, where the hedges and banks, by confining the traffic to one track, had brought the roads into such an abominable state that they could be used as a potent argument against the enclosure system. Fitzherbert tries to meet the objection by suggesting that fenced-in lanes should be used only where the ground is stony and dry, and that where it is soft 'at every hedge that goeth overthwart the highway, there to make a gate. . . . And then hath every man the whole close to ride, carry or go in as they had before'.[3] Wherever possible the traffic trampled out a wide verge of land 'thrown in, as it were, for an overplus to the highway'. In Sussex especially Defoe says he had seen 'the road, 60 to a hundred yards broad, lie from side to side all poached with cattle, the land of no manner benefit, and yet no going with a horse but at every step up to the shoulders, full of sloughs and holes and covered with standing water'.[4]

In the open-farming districts the traveller was free to pick his way to a much greater extent, but the result often was that the line of the road evaporated in an abstract right of way. This year the approach to the village might be straight forward across the fallow; but next year the fallow (following the usual rotation) might have been ploughed in long strips separated by balks or furrow leys, and the traveller might have to make a

[1] *Memoir of Colonel John Birch* (Camd. Soc.), p. 186.

[2] *History of the Life of Thomas Ellwood*, ed. C. Crump, 1900, p. 6.

[3] *Surveyenge*, Ch. XL.

[4] Defoe. *Essay on Projects*, 1697.

wide detour to reach his destination. A witness before the Star Chamber in the reign of James I testified that 'sometymes when the common feilds of Ladbrooke (in Warwickshire) lay open, the passengers . . . did in their jornies . . . passe and goe over the said comon feilds now and then upon one furrow ley and sometymes uppon another furrow ley as they would, but they did notwithstanding usually keepe neare one place.' He said that 'passengers doe the like in other common feilds', but nevertheless gave it as his opinion 'that there is and may be a high and comon way through such places'.[1] No doubt he was right, but it was evidently difficult in such districts even for the local farmers to say exactly where the road lay, and for the stranger it must often have been impossible. 'Travellers know no highwaies in the common fields' complains an agriculturist of the period, and much land was 'spoiled and trampled down in all wide roads where coaches and carts take liberty to choose for their best advantage.' The tendency of the traffic to 'fan out' wherever possible was particularly noticeable over heaths and commons. Arthur Young, writing in 1760, could remember the time when carriages approaching Norwich from the south 'would sometimes be a mile abreast of each other in pursuit of the best track'. Carriers crossing Salisbury Plain in 1689 were 'about two miles apart' when they were caught in a blizzard. Travellers to Brigg in Lincolnshire were guided by a land lighthouse; and those benighted on their way to Barton on Humber listened for the tolling of a bell.[2]

Evidently then, it was to the interest of the agricultural community that a thoroughfare, where it existed, should be kept clear. Nobody expected it to be good going. Indeed it seems to have been generally accepted in some districts that the worst possible way between two given points was along the common road. But as long as it was free from certifiable obstructions, and not demonstrably an impassable slough, it enabled Tom Touchy to take the law of any man who trespassed on the land adjoining. And to many a remote and stagnant and self-supporting village this was its sole value. The inhabitants did not use it themselves. They did not want to go anywhere. They were sometimes quite ignorant even of the name of a parish six miles

[1] *Star Chamber Proc.:* James I, 68, file 3.

[2] Prothero. *The Pioneers and Progress of English Farming*, 1888, pp. 44, 56.

farther along the road.[1] As far as they were concerned it was simply a strip abandoned to the stranger-public in return for their undisturbed occupation of the fields on either side.

Regarded in this light, the road was not likely to make any serious call upon their energy or invention, and the statutory repairs to it were usually undertaken in a purely agricultural spirit. The commonest method was simply to plough up the two edges of the track, throwing the earth inwards, and then level the surface with a harrow. A refinement consisted in filling up the ruts with stones or brushwood. Sometimes the whole surface was covered with gravel or broken stones; but this must have meant a good deal of heavy carting, and can only have been possible where carts were easily available. In general the process consisted in filling up the worst holes with something solid, and throwing back upon the surface the mud and gravel that the year's traffic had displaced.

Now as long as it had nothing more serious to bear in winter than packhorse traffic, even a road of this kind might remain passable;[2] for packhorse trains, by picking their way and avoiding the tracks of their predecessors, distributed the gross weight that the road had to take pretty evenly over its surface. But once a gang of maltsters' carts or clothiers' waggons had ploughed its way down such a road in wet weather, the deep ruts, widened by frost and surface-water, soon engulfed any surface dressing that might have been used upon it, and in a low-lying stretch converted the whole road into one protracted slough, in which pack-horses were certain to be bogged and foot passengers might even be drowned.[3] When this stage was reached the highway ceased to be passable except by waggons with teams powerful enough to drag them through 'on their bellies', and the small farmers, dairywomen and huxters who had been in the habit of taking their wares to market on horse-back by that route, were compelled either to set up waggons for themselves, or to become the clients of those who possessed them. It is to this breakdown of the roads that we may probably attribute the appearance of those 'long waggons' carrying

[1] *H.M. Com.* Clements, p. 222; and compare *Diary of Celia Fiennes*, ed. Griffiths, p. 81.

[2] W. Marshall. *Rural Economy of the Midland Counties*, 1796, I, 43. See Note 04.

[3] *Diary of Ralph Thoresby*, 1830, I, 295; and see Kemp's *Nine Days Wonder*, 1600, for the slough near Chelmsford which he tried to jump.

'passengers and commodities' which Stow mentions under the year 1564. Nobody travelled by them who could possibly avoid it: even Verney's housemaids felt entitled to demand pad-nags, 'the very name of a waggon was soe offensive to them'. They are a sign that the growing commercial traffic had brought some of the main roads into such a condition that they were no longer fit for the private traveller, and could be safely navigated only by professional waggoners with very powerful teams.

To give precise dates for a process which was in its nature gradual and cumulative is impossible, but this appearance of a wheeled passenger traffic in 1564 may perhaps be taken to mark the moment when the demands made upon the Elizabethan roads had become definitely greater than they could bear without a properly metalled surface, and when therefore the skilled services of professional carriers had become practically indispensable. Until road-surfaces could be strengthened, as they were at last by the Turnpike Acts from 1663 onwards, the progress could only be from bad to worse. The palliatives tried from time to time by the Stuart governments were quite ineffective, and in some cases certainly aggravated the evils they were supposed to cure. The proclamation of 1618, for instance, which forbade the use of heavy waggons altogether, and limited the load of a cart to one ton, was, for lack of machinery to ensure that the weight restriction was observed, positively mischievous. It simply tempted the carrier to load upon two wheels what ought to have been carried on four, and trust that the paucity of weighing machines would enable him to get by with it. A great deal could be done with English carts. The Duke of Wurtembourg was much struck by their size and capacity, and says that they would carry nearly as much as a waggon.[1] If so, they must have been, as the carriers themselves argued, far more destructive to an unmetalled road.

Another and later expedient was to encourage the use of broad wheels, in the hope that they would prevent or mitigate the formation of ruts. A proclamation of 1662 prescribed four inches as the minimum breadth for cart and waggon wheels; but it had to be withdrawn. The ruts already existed; and every waggoner knew that until they could be filled in, a narrow wheel travelled best and took the least out of his team. Hence while

[1] *England as seen by Foreigners*, ed. Rye, p. 14.

theorists continued to advocate the use of broad wheels, the practical wainwright (if we may judge by seventeenth-century illustrations) took pains to make them as narrow as possible. Not that he expected his handiwork to solve the traffic problem altogether. The moment was sure to come when even with the narrowest wheels a waggon would stick fast. But he provided for this contingency by equipping the narrow rim with iron bolt-heads or cogs, which protruded about an inch and gave a purchase in a difficult place when the waggoner had to put his shoulder to the wheel.[1] Granted the conditions there can be no doubt that these 'shod' wheels were a thoroughly practical invention from the waggoner's point of view. But meanwhile the narrow rims cut the ruts deeper where the ground was soft, and the iron cogs smashed and tore it up where it happened to be hard: so much so that towns, such as Bristol and Bury St Edmunds, which were trying to get their streets pitched, were obliged to prohibit the use of these 'shod' carts within the city boundaries.[2] They remained the bane of English traffic until the eighteenth century, when the Turnpike companies taxed them out of existence.

The effect of this growing traffic problem was to maintain and even to intensify the social and intellectual contrast between London and the provinces. The spirit of national unity fostered by Elizabeth's government and the successful contest with Spain had found a focus and a rallying point in the life of the capital. Here the spectacle of English wealth and English power, English law and English genius, might be seen not in dim vision or hopeful outline but as a thing achieved, solid and incontrovertible. Here were the beginnings of a social sense that ignored the old class distinctions, and of an intellectual freemasonry that drew together under the same starry heaven of wit the nobly born exquisite and the bricklayer's son. But this dazzling scene was becoming the more inaccessible the brighter it shone. A widening circle of mud and misery, caused by those very activities that gave the city its wealth and prestige, tended to insulate the capital from the life and thought of the country as a whole. A hundred miles from London they were still living in the

[1] See Note 05.
[2] *H.M. Com. Bury St Edmund's*, p. 141; Latimer, *Annals of Bristol* (seventeenth century), p. 58.

fifteenth century; two hundred miles away they were hardly out of the fourteenth. While Ben Jonson was refining upon points of scholarship at the Devil Tavern Sir Thomas Metcalfe of Wensleydale was laying siege to Raydall House with forty armed retainers; blazing away at the windows as though the War of the Roses was still in full swing;[1] and while fashionable congregations listened to the theological subtleties of a Sanderson or a Jeremy Taylor, an old man at Cartmel Fell was assuring his minister that he had indeed 'heard of that man you speak of (Jesus Christ) once at a play at Kendall, called Corpus Christi play, where there was a man on a tree, and blood ran down'.[2]

To bridge this enormous gulf many things were needed besides better roads—better education, an effective journalism and a more regular system of communications. Meanwhile the carrier did what he could. For more than a century he was the community's sole champion against its inveterate enemies, the wind and the rain. While the citizen took his evening pipe, and the tired farmer dozed by his fire, the carrier's gangs were still splashing thigh-deep through Mimm's Wash, or unpinning the wheels of their waggons to haul them one by one out of Dunchurch Lane; or their clanging pack-trains were vanishing into the wintry heights of the Pennines, there to plod on, hour after hour, along tracks known only to the curlews, until at last their bells would be heard again on Hartside, bringing news from London down the long zig-zag path into Melmerby and the Valley of the Lune.

For most country dwellers the carrier was the only regular means of contact with the outside world, and the recurring freshets of news that he brought stirred the sleeping pool of local opinion like the return of the tide, enabling its inhabitants to glow momentarily with a sense of the open sea. He was also, no less, the channel of rumour, and must often have done something to foment that extraordinary propensity to groundless panic which seems to have afflicted most country places in the seventeenth century. 'To tell news after the carrier' had become a proverbial way of describing a futile undertaking. The carrier had told all there was, and sometimes a good deal more. 'Simondshall news' was what they called it in Gloucestershire.

[1] *Journal of Nicholas Assheton*, 1617–18 (Chetham Soc.).
[2] *Life of John Shaw* (Surtees Soc., 1875), p. 138.

> The clothiers, horsecarriers and wainmen of this hun(weekly frequent London, knowinge by ancient custome th question, after welcome home from London, is 'What London?' doe usually gull us with feigned inventions, devised by them upon those downes; which wee either then suspecting upon the report, or after findinge false, wee cry out 'Simondsall newes'. A generall speach betweene every cobler's teeth.[1]

But this was peace-time fooling. At moments of crisis when the public was terrified by rumours of a hideous Popish Plot, or of a disbanded Irish army storming across the country and burning folk in their beds, the arrival of the London carrier on his usual day, reporting all quiet on the road, must have had a steadying effect. If the carrier could keep his day, things could not be so bad; and thus his stubborn figure, plodding along the roads which most of them would never travel, and through regions which they hardly knew by name, became the symbol and almost the assurance of an immutable order:–

> Obedient to the Moon he kept his date
> In course reciprocal, and had his fate
> Linked to the mutual flowings of the Seas.[2]

How natural that when one of these timid stay-at-homes was obliged for some reason to undertake a journey, he should have put himself in the charge of this stolid Mercury with his *caduceus* of hazel-twig, and travelled with the carrier.

[1] J. Smyth. *Lives of the Berkeleys*, III, 30.
[2] Milton. *On the University Carrier* (the second set of verses).

IV

Travel with the Carrier

TRAVEL with the carrier was so slow and tiresome that people of means and condition seldom stooped to it, but it had great advantages for the man or woman who would otherwise have had to travel alone. The carrier knew every inch of his road, which might, for miles at a stretch, be a confusion of straggling tracks with never a sign-post, and no light but the glowworm after sundown; he could tell where the floods were likely to be out, and what detour must be made, and which fields were fallow or newly reaped and open to a rider; and at his inn at night there would usually be an ordinary on the carrier's day, where the traveller could take his meal without the trouble of ordering it, and so get to bed early. The expense too was variable. A needy young man like William Lilly could pay the carrier to take his bundle, and trudge the whole way on foot.[1] A young woman might be found a seat on a packhorse, and charged as half a pack,[2] or perhaps among the bales in the waggon, if there was no risk of the load's shifting. Loads did sometimes shift, and young women had been smothered;[3] so she would probably feel happier if the carrier used one of those covered waggons fitted with seats for passengers, which were safer, no doubt, if less comfortable. Charged as half a pack from

[1] William Lilly. *History of his Life and Times*, 1714, p. 6.
[2] D. Scott. *Bygone Cumberland and Westmoreland*, 1899, p. 217.
[3] See Note 06.

Oswestry to London (120 miles) she would have to pay 4*s*. 6*d*. and something for her food: say 10*s*. altogether.[1] 'But this kind of journeying', says Fynes Morrison, 'is so tedious, by reason they must take waggon very early, and come very late to their Innes, as none but women and people of inferiour condition, or strangers (as Flemmings with their wives and servants) use to travel in this sort.' The social prejudice against it was strengthened by the fact that the London procuresses haunted the carriers' terminus in Smithfield in the hope of picking up country girls, so that to say of a young woman that she had 'come up with the carrier' was to make an imputation.[2] It was no doubt for this reason that 'the very name of a waggon was so offensive' to Verney's respectable housemaids, and that they pressed so firmly for 'padd-nags'.

These too could be provided by most carriers, who, says Fynes Morrison, 'let horses from Citie to Citie, with caution that the passenger must lodge in their Inne, that they may looke to the feeding of their horse; and so they will for some five or sixe dayes journey let him a horse, and find the horse meate themselves for some twenty shillings'. The Oxford carrier was required by his contract to keep a dozen such horses for the use of scholars at 6*d*. a day,[3] and Hobson of Cambridge is said to have kept forty. They could be used without loss of face by any young gentleman who could borrow some riding boots and contrive a pair of 'vamps', or boot-socks, out of his table-cloth.[4] It is true that some very elegant young gentlemen at the University were allowed by indulgent parents to keep horses of their own. But the dons were dead against it. 'I understand', says the Tutor in *The Guardian's Instruction* 1688, that you have brought him up a fine Padd to keep here for his health's sake; now I will tell you the use of an Horse in Oxford, and then doe as you think fit. The Horse must be kept at an Ale-house or an Inn, and he must have leave to go once every day to see him eat Oats, because the Master's eye makes him fat; and it will not be Genteel to go often to an House and spend nothing; and then there may be some danger of the Horse growing resty

[1] See Note 07.

[2] See Note 08.

[3] *Register of the University of Oxford*, ed. Clark, II, 315; *The Diary of Thomas Crosfield*, ed. Boas, p. 7.

[4] *The Life of Sir George Radcliffe*, ed. Whitaker, 1810, p. 67.

if he be not used often, so that you must give him leave to go to Abingdon once every week to look out of the Tavern Window, and see the Maids sell Turnips: and in one month or two come home with a surfeit of poisoned Wine, and save any farther charges by dying: and then you will be troubled to send for your horse again.' The pressure of these official views brought the carrier's hacks more elegant customers than they might otherwise have had, and they acquired that sort of prestige which is always accorded to monumental incapacity.

'Thou paltry fellow', shouted the Post who had had to give way to a Cambridge scholar, riding one of Hobson's monuments, 'dost thou not see I am a Poste'? 'And thou ignorant fellow', replied the scholar, 'dost thou not see that I ride *upon* a poste'?[1] A good rider could sometimes get them going. Seth Ward, as a Cambridge undergraduate, 'riding in company of others to London or elsewhere, frequently chang'd horses with those who could not make theirs go, and with those tir'd jades led the way'.[2] But even with a good pace-maker they were slow, and often seemed slower than they really were. 'Twelve scholars riding together, one of them said, "My Masters, let us ride faster". "Why", quoth another, "methinkes we ride a good pace; I'll warrant it is four mile an hour". "Alas!" said the first, "what is four mile an hour amongst all us?" '[3]

But, as Hobson used to tell them on these occasions, 'they would come time enough to London if they did not ride too fast'. 'How many a man', says Lord North (who had been at Cambridge in Hobson's time), 'hath tyred his horse by riding a little too fast, who might otherwise have come well to his journies end'.[4] Besides, was it not well known that horse-hire 'by journey' was restricted to 'journey's pace', and that any carrier's horse caught 'running the gallopp' might be impounded by a Government postmaster? Therefore *lente, lente, curre Hobsonis eque.*

Since the pace was bound to be slow poor hacks were usually provided, but in most carriers' stables the traveller had some freedom of choice. Not, however, in Hobson's. 'When a man

[1] John Taylor. *Works*, 1630, p. 184.
[2] Walter Pope. *The Life of Seth, Lord Bishop of Salisbury*, 1697, p. 90.
[3] John Taylor. *Works*, 1630, p. 186.
[4] Lord North. *The Forest of Varieties*, 1645 (4 Nov. 1637).

came for a horse he obliged him to take the horse which stood next the stable door; so that every customer was alike served according to his chance, and every horse ridden with the same justice'.[1] The solid basis if this tradition is the fact that the University carriers were exempted from purveyance (at Cambridge by the charter of 1561, at Oxford by an Order in Council of 1575), and were therefore not bound to supply horses to meet a post-warrant, or to bother their heads with the stipulation which it always contained for 'hable and sufficient' horses: a phrase which invited controversy. In Hobson's stable you took what you got, and the fact that this was remembered clearly indicates that the custom in most stables was different. But freedom of choice probably meant little. The range of choice was limited, and a philosophic mood was required in the traveller who rode at 'journey's pace'. It was quite possible to read a book; John Wesley read many a book as he rode about England, and a scholar in the saddle might become so deeply absorbed as to forget where he was.

'My cousin told me when she was first married to her husband Marche, as she rode behind him she slipt down, and he left her behind; never lookt back to take her up; so she went so long afoot that she took it so unkindly that she thought never to have come again to him, but to have sought a service in some unknown place. But he took her at last'.[2]

It was one of the advantages, for an absent minded man, of riding with a carrier's gang that if an accident of this kind happened, someone would be sure to draw his attention to it. It was undoubtedly the safest mode of travel, and the misadventures attending it were, for the most part, too trivial to be recorded. But the following newsletter, printed in 1685, serves as a reminder that the hazards of the road were serious, and that the responsibilities of a carrier might suddenly become very heavy.

'On Tuesday, 23rd December, 1684, the weather being cold and freezing, there likewise happened a terrible and certainly the most dreadful storm that hath in these nations been heard of in the memory of man. . . . The carriers from London to Exeter, Taunton, Shaftesbury, Bath, and Wells &c, going as usual out of London on Saturday, and particularly the 20th

[1] *The Spectator*, No. 509.

[2] Manningham's *Diary* (Camd. Soc.), p. 14.

December, and in pursuance of their respective journeys, being, on Tuesday the 23rd, to pass the downs on this side Salisbury; such of them as escaped, and are since returned to London, do relate . . . that the wind being all day north east and violently cold, about two in the afternoon it began to snow very fast, and held on till two or three the next morning, the wind continuing fierce, and blowing it in such heaps that in some places the snow lay as high as a house-top, in others the ground scarcely covered; which so altered the roads, especially upon the downs and plains, that although some of them had weekly used the same roads for thirty or forty years together, none of the said carriers could that night either find the way to their inns, or any towns where they might get shelter, but themselves, their passengers, and horses, forced to wander about, till many of them were frozen to death who, before the storm began, were hearty and healthful; each of the said carriers labouring and being lost several miles distant from the other.

'Mr Matthews, the carrier of Shaftesbury, had his unfortunate lot within 56 miles of London, two miles on this side Stockbridge, who, albeit he escaped with life, yet his hands are frozen up that he hath lost the use of them, and two of his horses died with extremity of cold upon the downs that very night. Mr Morris, the younger, carrier to Exeter, also Mr Clark, the elder, who carries to Shaftesbury, Yeovil and other parts, with their horses and passengers, were lost upon the down six miles beyond Stockbridge, there in like manner wandering all night to and again, by continued action were preserved alive. Mr Collins, the Taunton carrier, and Mr —, the carrier to Bath and Wells, (who) with their gangs of horses and passengers, travelled that day about two miles distant each from other, were passing between Andover and Amesbury, and when first lost, judged they might want five or six miles of Amesbury. The Wells carrier being foremost, had two of his company frozen to death, viz. his own son, a youth about 13 or 14, and a young man, a passenger, aged about 20 years; which persons were not parted from the rest, nor smothered in the snow, but absolutely frozen to death as they rode or walked along in company. The distressed carrier's bowels yearning when he saw his son grow stiff and faint, (he) got him up and carried him till he died in his arms, and after he was dead carried him on horseback until extremity of cold forced him to let him drop upon the down and leave him.

'Neither had Mr Collins, who carries to Taunton and Tiverton, less misfortune. A man and his wife, two hearty ancient people, being of his passengers, and riding on single horses, although very healthy and well in the morning, and cheerful in the afternoon, yet by the continued cold and the strangglling of the poor horses, or by their own growing too feeble to manage them, lost sight of the gang and wandered by themselves, till at length they lay down and died, one at the feet of the other. Mr Collins, himself and servants, when within three miles of Amesbury, happened upon a parish where they hired a guide for ten shillings, who undertook to lead the bell-horse, and conducted them a mile and a half of the three; when going faster than they could follow, Mr Collins begged of him not to go faster than they were able to come with the other horses; but the guide, alleging that his own life was in danger, kept on his pace and got safe to the Bear Inn at Amesbury by nine o'clock at night. Mr Collins, his servants and horses, wandering till six in the morning, and then discovering an old barn, broke into it for shelter till daylight. One of his said servants is like to lose the use of his limbs, and Mr Collins, with the rest, merely (under God) by violent labour and bustling saved their lives.

'The servant of Lady Fiennes, of Newton Tony in the county of Wilts, having been that day at Salisbury market, on his return with a cart and two horses lost himself on the same down, and having tied his fore horse's head to the cart, was found dead near them by 8 o'clock that evening, and being within half a mile of Amesbury, the servants of the Bear Inn, coming out to look for the carriers, found him in the manner aforesaid. A shopkeeper living near Chalke, a place in those parts, also perished in coming from Salisbury market. Six or seven country people in passing from Chard to Ilminster, though but three or four miles distant, were by the way frozen to death. One Mr Knight of Yeovil, in a letter to a friend in this city, affirms that about thirty people, from that town and parts adjacent, that went the same day to markets or after other concerns, were not heard of, except some few found dead. About Tiverton many in like manner perished as they went from markets. Between Plymouth and Exeter many were smothered in the snow.

'From almost every part of the western road we have the same dreadful news, which all happened upon the very same day, and the truth thereof ready to be testified by hundreds that are since returned to this city, besides the carriers herein mentioned, who are themselves men of great credit.'[1]

[1] A pamphlet by George Larkin 1685, reprinted by Miss F. Child in *The Spinster at home in the Close of Salisbury*, 1844.

V

The Common Carrier

ALTHOUGH Town carriers had been travelling the roads since the fourteenth century[1] their trade had never been clearly recognized as one of the 'common callings', and until nearly the end of the seventeenth century the liabilities of a carrier were not, or not consistently, distinguished from those of any man who might happen to carry a parcel for a friend. He was simply a 'bailee': that is, a man who, in taking charge of another man's goods, assumes an absolute liability for them to the owner, and in the mean time has a legal remedy against anyone who seeks to destroy them or take them from his possession. He is responsible for all loss or damage against which he has this legal remedy. Since he cannot bring an action against Providence or sue a foreign power 'acts of God and of the King's enemies' rid him of his liability. But he had a legal remedy against loss by fire, for until 1708 an action lay against any person in whose house a fire broke out; and he had a remedy against highway robbery, for if the thief escaped the hue and cry the robbed person was empowered by the Statute of Westminster to recover from the hundred in which the robbery had occurred.[2] Against these two risks, therefore, of fire and robbery the carrier, as a bailee, was regarded as an insurer, unless he had expressly stipulated that he was not. The principle was established in

[1] Thorold Rogers. *History of Prices*, I, 660.
[2] See O. W. Holmes. *The Common Law*, 1881, p. 187 *et seq.*

Southcote's case (1601), which was quoted as a precedent throughout the seventeenth century. Southcote had entrusted goods to Bennet for delivery to a certain address, and Bennet had agreed to take them, but in transit they were stolen by one of Bennet's servants. The court found Bennet liable because, although it had apparently been a friendly transaction and no 'reward' had been agreed between them, Bennet had not made special conditions. And Lord Coke, in his note on this case, laid special emphasis on this point.

> 'Note reader, it is good policy for him who takes any goods to keep, to take them in a special manner, *scil* "to keep them as he keeps his own goods", or "to keep them the best that he can at the peril of the party", or "if they happen to be stolen or purloined, that he shall not answer for them"; for he that accepteth them ought to take them in such or the like manner, or otherwise he may be charged by his general acceptance.'[1]

So far the carrier's position was clear.

But the difficulty was that a man who followed 'a common calling' was held at this time to be precluded from making a 'special acceptance' of that kind. A 'common innkeeper' at that time could not take charge of a traveller's luggage 'at the owner's risk'. He had to accept full liability for it. So had a 'common farrier' for the horse that he took to shoe or physic. If therefore a carrier could be shown (by his methods of business or other evidence) to be in fact a 'common' carrier, there was a growing tendency for the courts to maintain that he was 'a bailee of the first class'; that is, a bailee who must accept full liability for the goods he carried. 'He is bound to answer for the goods at all events', declared Chief Justice Holt in the case of *Coggs* v *Bernard* 1703. 'The law charges this person thus intrusted to carry goods, against all events but acts of God, and of the enemies of the King. For though the force be never so great, as if an irresistible multitude of people should rob him, nevertheless he is chargeable'. And from this it appears that the 'common' carrier (if rightly so called) had no means of escape. He could not refuse to carry valuables. He could be obliged to carry even bags of money unless he could 'assign a particular reason'. All that he could do in such cases was to charge a special rate. And even then if a customer, evading his rate, packed £100

[1] Coke's *Reports*, IV, 83^{b}.

in a parcel of tobacco and said nothing about it, the carrier could be held liable for that £100—or perhaps for £98, if the court was in a good humour, and allowed him the rate that ought to have been paid.[1] To guard against nasty surprises of this kind he had to secure from his customer a declaration that money was not included in his parcel, and if it was, of the amount. This at least enabled him to calculate his liabilities on his load. But it did nothing to limit them. So long as his customers were prepared to declare the nature of the goods, and to pay the appropriate rate, he had to take what they offered, and he might easily find himself approaching Gads Hill with money and valuables amounting to a sum which he could not possibly repay if the highwaymen got them.

This was a serious matter not only for the carrier himself but also for those who employed him, and corporations usually took care, in appointing their Town carrier, that he should be a man of substance, engaged in some other trade as well as carrying. But since complete security was in the circumstances impossible, they seem to have been willing to ease the position for the carrier by coming to a tacit compromise about this business of declaring values.

The law which held the common carrier responsible for loss by robbery was in fact simply an application of the general law of bailments. But it was popularly regarded as a safeguard against faked robbery, 'for else', said Chief Justice Holt, who gave this popular view his action in 1703, 'these carriers might have an opportunity of undoing all persons that had any dealings with them, by combining with thieves &c, and yet doing it in such a clandestine manner as would not be possible to be discovered'. But to insure against collusion of this kind it was clearly unnecessary that the carrier should be held liable for every pennyworth of his load. It would suffice if he were held liable for such proportion of its value as would make collusion in a bogus robbery an unprofitable enterprise. Thus if he were entrusted with £500, it might be sufficient to hold him responsible for £400, because by the time he had shared the odd £100 with a number of 'men in buckram', he would not have enough to compensate him for the disorganization of his business and the very real risk to his neck.

[1] *Kenrig* v *Eggleston*, 1648.

It seems to have become the practice, therefore, to declare only a portion of the sum entrusted to a carrier, and to pay the special rate only on the amount declared. It suited the honest carrier, who was glad enough to reduce the gross sum for which he was liable on his load; and it suited the customer, who, in default of complete security, wanted to reduce the amount of the special rate that he had to pay.

An instance of such an arrangement is to be seen in the case of *Tyly* v *Morrice* (1699). Morrice, the Exeter carrier, had been robbed on Hounslow Heath of sums amounting to £850; but only £500 had been declared and paid for at the special rate by the senders. Now it is difficult to suppose that a man would accept liability for £500 without satisfying himself that the bags contained at least that amount, and in the process of making sure he could hardly have failed to discover that they contained a great deal more. It was no doubt because Morrice was so obviously privy to the arrangement that the plaintiffs were emboldened to sue him for the whole amount. But the court held that he was liable only for the sum specified in his contract, which he had already paid up, and Morrice was thus successful in throwing back upon his customers part of the risk which the law of bailments imposed upon him. That he was not the first common carrier to connive at such an arrangement may safely be assumed. Indeed, unless the practice had been known to be common, it is difficult to believe that the suit would have been brought against him at all.

It is clear that by this date (1699) the system of charging a special rate on money declared had become a real safeguard to the carrier, but it did little or nothing to reduce the risk of loss. It was sometimes argued that for the extra money he ought to supply an armed guard. But as a practical man who had to travel lonely roads at all hours week after week, he knew that if it once came to shooting the odds were overwhelmingly in favour of the highwayman, and further, that any carrier who had the misfortune to kill one of a gang would be wise to change his occupation. What the special rate really secured was simply that the carrier knew in which packet the money was, and would take care not to let it out of his sight on the journey. But this in itself might be a source of danger, by providing the highwayman or his confederates with just the clue they needed. It is to be remembered that a highwayman had to work in a hurry if he was to escape the hue and cry, and that to rummage ten or a dozen packs in the hope of finding a bag of money might take him more time than he could afford. On the whole, therefore, many people thought that the safest way of sending money was to hide it in a parcel of merchandise and say nothing about it; and this method was adopted by responsible officials. In November 1582 Alderman Martin writes about money to be sent to Bristol for the service in Ireland, 'If it be Burghley's good liking a sum of money may be delivered into the charge of a carrier, but packed up in such a manner, amongst other things, as he shall suppose it to be merchandises for that place as are usually carried hence'.[1] In the same gambling spirit Robert Woodford, Steward of Northampton, who had collected £70 in London for the relief of plague victims in his home town in 1638, notes in his diary

> June 21. Went to the carryer endeavouring to sende downe my money, but could not under 10*s*, so I put the gold in my boots and prayed unto the Lord to direct me.[2]

When the sums were not too large a carrier of good credit could often disburse what was required, and recover from his customer on his return, thus avoiding the necessity of transporting cash altogether. The Purefoys in the early eighteenth century did much of their London shopping through the Buckingham carrier in this way, and one can not doubt that many seventeenth century carriers were able to offer the same convenience.

Whether the carriers insured their loads I have not found evidence to show, but it can hardly have been a common practice. In a country almost entirely unpoliced an easy system of insurance would have increased the risk of collusion in faked robbery, and the rates would have had to be fixed very high. The carrier was already protected against robbery by the Statute of Westminster, and had a similar legal remedy in case of loss by fire. As for loss or damage by flood-water, which must indeed have been a serious risk on some routes, he might reasonably hope to succeed in the plea that flood was 'an Act of God' for which no man could be held responsible.

[1] *H.M. Com. Cecil II*, Letter of Alderman Martin, Nov. 1582.
[2] *Diary of Robert Woodford* (*H.M. Com. 9th Report*, Appendix, p. 498).

On the whole there can have been little inducement to insure. Some carriers, however, apparently thought it worth their while to pay protection money to the highwaymen. William Nevinson, the celebrated Tory highwayman who was hanged in 1684, is said to have exacted a regular toll from Whig carriers and drovers using the north road. But he was a somewhat exceptional scoundrel who had managed to convince the public that he was lucky (always a strong card in the hands of a crook), and he operated on a road passing through much thinly populated country where the hue and cry was difficult to raise. It is doubtful whether on the more frequented southern roads near London the highwaymen were lucky long enough to exact this kind of blackmail.

VI

The Private Carrier

But in spite of such mitigations and contrivances the liabilities of a 'common carrier' remained heavy under Stuart law, and it is probable that only the men in a big way of business could afford to assume the title. Fortunately for the smaller men the status and duties of a carrier had never been made the subject of a statutory declaration. An innkeeper was by a statute of Henry IV's reign a 'common innkeeper', and the writ against him alleged 'the law and custom of England'; but the carrier had never in the same way been declared a 'common carrier', and it was not until the seventeenth century was well advanced that the lawyers began to insinuate 'the custom of England' in attempting to define his obligations. There was no government tax on carriers, and no general license which a carrier as such must hold. Many corporations taxed and licensed the carters who plied in their own streets, and in 1630 Dame Alice Wigmore was granted a patent for an 'incorporation of carriers, footposts, hackney coachmen, badgers, kidders, laders, polterers, maltsters and drovers' who were to wear a 'badge of silver, . . . and the payment for such badges to go to the petitioner for three years'.[1] This might have developed into a useful system of registration, if it could have been put into effect; but it seems to have been abortive. The only license which a carrier who carried foodstuffs was practically bound to take out was that prescribed by the

[1] *C.S.P. Dom.* (L629–31).

Act of 1571 for the 'badger, kidder or carrier of corn, cattle, butter, cheese or other victuals'; but this was merely a safeguard against the cornering of foodstuffs, and the possession of such a license did not settle the question whether the holder was a 'common' carrier or not. That remained simply a question of fact. Had he in fact been at everyone's beck and call? Had he for instance, accepted letters and parcels from unknown persons to be left at places that he passed on his way home? If he had, he was in fact a common carrier, whatever license he might hold and whatever title he might prefer. But if he had not, he escaped the general obligation implicit in the title, and the extent of his liability would have to be determined by the facts in the particular case.

Hence it was possible for the man of slender resources to gain a footing in the carrying trade without shouldering responsibilities too heavy for him. If he could make good the claim, or keep up the fiction, that he was merely a private person obliging certain neighbours, or that he was in some sense their factor or agent, paid for a job of work, he was free to accept goods for transport on special terms—'to keep them as he keeps his own', or 'to keep them the best he can at the peril of the party'; which meant that he could not be held liable as a bailee for loss by fire, robbery or any other unavoidable accident, and that the worst he had to fear was a civil action for negligence. Everything depended on keeping up the fiction (if fiction it were) that he was not a 'common' carrier; and at the 'home' end of his beat this was probably easy enough to arrange. So long as he was prepared to take their goods regularly to market his neighbours in a small country place would call him anything he liked. It was at the other end, in London, that his difficulties were likely to arise. How was he to get a profitable return load without accepting the goods of strangers, and so queering his own pitch? Something might be done, perhaps, by letting it be known that all parcels should be left with Mr. Blank, landlord of The Feathers, and insisting that he accepted them purely to oblige Mr. Blank. But would Mr. Blank play? And even if he did, would the device wash? There is no doubt that many carriers were very nervous about it. When John Taylor went round the inn-yards in 1637, collecting information for his *Carrier's Cosmography*, he was surprised to find himself regarded with great suspicion, treated to 'harsh and unsavoury answers', and sometimes denied the information that he sought. But it was only to be expected. The fact that a man had allowed his name to appear in a public advertisement of this kind would have been taken as conclusive evidence in a court of law that he was a 'common carrier', and liable as such. In short Taylor's publication threatened to destroy the careful fiction under which many of these men were gaining their livelihood; and to their anxiety on this point is perhaps to be attributed the rather curious fact that, at a time when the relations between tradesman and client were so close and personal, and proper names were so freely used, the *Carrier's Cosmography* does not contain a single carrier's name.

How many of them were in the proper sense common carriers is now, and probably was then, impossible to say. Those who took up or delivered indiscriminately at places lying on their route could hardly have escaped the designation, and Taylor's preface makes it clear that this was common practice on all the main roads. But some of them could probably have protected themselves by their agreements with towns or public bodies. The carrier appointed by the University of Oxford, for instance, is described in his contract as an 'officer and common servant of the University', and as such he was probably free to make 'special acceptance' of the goods he carried. Similarly Thomas Lucas of Ipswich, clothier, who in 1625 gives his bond that 'as town carrier' he will observe the orders of the general court, could probably have claimed to be a factor or agent, and not a common carrier, as long as he carried for none but freemen of the town.[1] But the majority would probably have been quite unable to say whether they were legally common carriers or not, for the facts might be highly complicated. A man who had a contract with a dairyman to take cheeses up to London, and made up his return load with anything he could get, was clearly a factor or agent on the up journey, but indistinguishable from a common carrier on his way home. If he varied these activities by taking his neighbours' eggs and butter to the next market-town and selling them on commission, he became *pro tem* a 'higgler'; and if he bought a load of barley there, and sold it on his return to the local maltster, he became what was called

[1] *H.M. Com. 9th Report*, Appendix, p. 260.

a 'badger'. Badger, higgler, carrier and factor—a handy man with a cart might be all these things in the course of a single month, and what he amounted to at the month's end was a matter for legal arithmetic.

There is no doubt that the provincial carrying trade, especially in the north and west, was very largely in the hands of men of this class: small farmers who lived to a great extent by barter, and used it as a means of getting some cash into the house; husbandmen whose holdings were insufficient for the support of their families, and young men who were sick of stagnating in a village, and saved up for a jagger pony as their successors now save up for a motor-bike. In the Quarter Sessions Records of the North Riding from 1625 to 1642 I find no mention of carriers as such, but during these years scores of men are presented for 'badging' (i.e. carrying foodstuffs or dealing in them) without a license. In Durham, and also in Somersetshire, large numbers of the country folk eked out their livelihood by peddling banister-loads of coal or charcoal; in Yorkshire by carrying the ore of the iron or lead mines; in north Worcestershire by taking horse-loads of rock-salt to the Severn barges. Wherever there was a trade in heavy goods that could employ packhorse traffic, large numbers of the country folk were sure to drift into the carrying business. In her minutely detailed study of seventeenth century Rydal Miss Armitt showed that nearly every 'statesman' or small farmer in the place was engaged at some time or other in the business of carrying goods, and that for several of them it became in the end their chief means of livelihood.

There is nothing at all surprising in this, for the work of a small carrier had affinities with what Henry Peacham called 'the most pleasing of all recreations', *viz* 'riding with a good horse and a good companion in the spring or summer season into the country, where the blossoms are on the trees and flowers in the fields, or when corn and fruit are ripe in autumn. What sweet and goodly prospects shall you have on both sides of you upon the way!—delicate green fields, low meadows, diversity of crystal streams, woody hills, parks with deer, hedgerows, orchards, fruit trees, churches, villages, the houses of gentlemen and husbandmen, several habits and faces, variety of country labours and exercises! If you happen, as often falleth out, to converse with countrymen of the place you shall find them for the most part understanding enough to give you satisfaction; and sometimes country maids and market wenches will give as unhappy answers as they are asked knavish and uncivil questions'.[1] One cannot doubt that the small carrier had plenty of fun on the roads in fine weather, and a much greater sense of freedom than could be attained by most working men.

But it was essential to his business that he should maintain close personal relations with his customers and put their convenience before his own. An ordinary common carrier in a big way of business, like Morrice of Exeter or Bradshaw of Leicester, would hand your letter to a porter in London and trouble no more about it; but the private carrier would deliver it with his own hand, as if he were your personal servant.

He would take apples and nuts to your small boys at their school, or make a detour to visit your eldest at Oxford, and bring back word of how he looked, and of what he was doing for exercise. He would even convey paternal reproofs, when required, and take it upon himself to advance, or not to advance, pocket-money.[2] To the freshmen, who were often lads of 14 or 15, the University carrier was a sort of general uncle. 'He is the student's joy and expectation', says Earle, 'and the most accepted guest, to whom they lend a willing hand to discharge him of his burden. His first greeting is commonly "Your friends are well"; then in a piece of gold delivers their blessing'.[3]

'I understand by my carrier', says one of these lads in 1625, 'that you are disposed to bestow a suit upon me'; and again, 'I hear by the carrier that our new orchard goes forward with great expedition'. Could he have some cakes and a cheese? 'I hope to receive them from you upon Saturday by this carrier, who is a very honest fellow, and hath promised me to call in our house always when he cometh into Norfolk, which is once a fortnight, and will bring letters or anything for me which you will send'.[4]

An 'honest fellow' of this kind was almost indispensable to the life of a remote country household, and might become in a real

[1] Henry Peacham. *The Worth of a Penny*, 1647.

[2] *Life of Sir George Radcliffe*, ed. Whitaker, 1810, p. 46.

[3] Earle. *Micro Cosmographie*, 1628 (Arber's Rpt., p. 36).

[4] Letter of William Gaudy, quoted by J. Venn. *Early Collegiate Life*, 1913, p. 207.

sense a friend of the family. Nothing was too confidential to be committed to his care. Letters that it would be unsafe to send by post (since the post was often opened) would be kept for the carrier, and if he failed to call in time for them, would be burnt.[1] My Lord Berkeley instructs his steward in London about arrangements for his son's marriage; my Lady, who has not been consulted in the matter, asks the same steward to let her know what is happening by the carrier—presumably a creature too humble and familiar with kitchen-entrances to catch his Lordship's eye.[2] But humble as he was, he could safely be trusted with twenty or thirty pounds to pay bills in town, and would faithfully deliver the signed receipts upon his return. If required he would even take a young girl up to London to seek a situation, and when she had got it, would look her up from time to time.[3] He would buy your hemp-seed for you, sell your surplus butter from the home farm, choose a barrel of oysters, take your razors to be ground or your watch to be repaired, keep you supplied with the gazettes and, of course, fetch your letters. Indeed he was quite wounded if anyone else was supposed capable of fetching your letters. In everything that he did for you he tried to keep up the rôle of the trusty retainer; and when the time came to settle accounts with him, you let him see that you regarded him in that light: paid for the goods he had carried or bought for you, settled the bill for the gazettes, and 'promised him a pair of old breeches for his letters', adding, if necessary, 'sixpence gratis to stop his mouth'.[4] It was all as pleasant and offhand as Father William could have wished.

But one important feature of this pleasant personal relationship was that the private carrier (or demi-carrier as he was sometimes called) did the whole errand himself, and could not delegate it. This, of course, was part of a trusty retainer's technique, but it arose inevitably from the limited nature of his liability. If a 'common carrier' accepted your parcel and delivered it to another person who lost it, you had an action against the carrier, and the carrier had an action against that person. But if a man in the position of your factor or servant did the same thing,

[1] *The Savile Correspondence*, p. 18.
[2] J. Smyth. *Lives of the Berkeleys*, II, 383.
[3] *Long Meg of Westminster*, 1584.
[4] *Journal of the Rev Giles Moore* (Sussex Arch. Soc., Vol. I).

you could not sue him, except for negligence, and he could not sue the person who had lost the parcel, having at law no shadow of possessory right in it. The action lay with you, as the owner, against the actual delinquent, who might be at the other end of England, and when you ran him to earth, might turn out to be just such a 'trusty retainer' as your own man, equally obliging, and equally wary of admitting his liability.

Thus public confidence in these men could never be strong enough to warrant their co-operating with each other and organizing their trade. If they could have pooled their resources and worked to a common time-table many towns might have had a carrier service to London two or three times a week instead of weekly or fortnightly, as seems to have been the rule. But the small men could not combine in this way without becoming 'common carriers', and most of the 'common carriers' could afford the title only because they enjoyed a virtual monopoly of carriage from a certain town, or over a certain route. There was therefore no inducement to combine. Waggoners of certain districts might join in a petition, and carriers of the same town might support each other at law. But anything in the nature of amalgamation was clearly impossible among men whose legal status and liabilities varied so greatly. They remained a crowd of independent competitors, travelling the same roads, often upon the same errands, and using collectively horses and gear sufficient to provide perhaps ten times as good a transport service under more favourable conditions.

VII

Thwarting the Highwayman

THIS waste of transport facilities was aggravated by a custom of the road which the carriers seem to have adopted for their protection. Throughout the seventeenth century the risks of highway robbery were greatest in the district immediately surrounding London, partly, no doubt, because it offered the most frequent opportunities, but chiefly because 'the largeness of the city and the little cognizance one takes of another' made it the best refuge for the robber and the readiest market for his loot. But the highwaymen operating in this area laboured under one serious disadvantage. They could not linger upon the scene of their exploit, but must pick a victim and decamp before news of their presence, spreading along the much frequented road, had roused the hue and cry. It is true that after the Civil War, when their numbers had been swelled by officers and men of the disbanded armies, they were sometimes able, by picketing the approaches and posting look outs, virtually to close a section of highroad for an hour or more, and plunder at their leisure. But this was a post war phenomenon. The highwaymen of the earlier half of the seventeenth century seem never to have worked in bands large enough for such 'hold ups', and usually appear as a handful of men in a desperate hurry.

It was therefore a sound policy for the carriers, and for those who travelled with them, to ride, not in close companies armed for defence, but in loose columns strung out along perhaps a mile or two of the road. This formation did not, of course, make it impossible that somebody would be robbed; but it made it practically certain that if one was robbed, the rest would for the time being escape. Jackson, the reformed highwayman whose *Recantation* was published in 1673,[1] is emphatic on this point. 'Shun that idle custom of bustling up all together, when you come near any place noted for robbing, for by this means you are all catched, like a covey in a net at once; for the rogues divide themselves and make several stands, and by this means they may set upon you before and behind; but if you ride about a hundred paces distant one from another, I'll warrant your safety; for they dare not set upon a scattered company, for fear that some escaping, the country should be alarmed, and so endanger their immediate taking'. This is advice to the private traveller; but the professional carriers understood the principle as well as the highwayman himself, and whenever possible travelled through the dangerous area in loose columns or companies. An analysis of Taylor's *Carrier's Cosmography* shows this clearly.

At various inns in Gracechurch Street were to be found carriers for Braintree, Dunmow, Coggeshall, Colchester and half a dozen other towns in Essex and Suffolk. These all came in on Thursday, and all left on Friday. The carriers for York, Doncaster and other Yorkshire places set out from the Belle Sauvage on Monday: those from Leeds, Wakefield and Halifax came to the Bear in Bassishaw on Wednesday. Those for Nantwich, Stafford, Chester, Shrewsbury, Denbigh, Bampton and Manchester all left town on Friday. So did the carriers for Blandford Bruton, Dorchester, Wells and Exeter, who lodged at the Rose. Other western carriers (Bath, Cheltenham, Tewkesbury and Winchcombe) who lodged at the Three Cups, and a Somersetshire group (Wells, Sherborne, Shaftesbury, Batcombe and Ivell) who lay at Jarrett's Hall, all took the road on Saturday. Some of these may be duplicates, and some may not have been in London every week; so that the groups may actually have been smaller than they appear. But the *Carrier's Cosmography* strongly suggests that although the practice may not have been universal, the custom of travelling in companies was common on all the main roads leading out of London.

It may be worth noting that during the civil war the carriers

[1] *Old Bookcollectors' Miscellany*, ed. Hindley, III, p. 43.

seem to have adopted different tactics which, nevertheless, illustrate the same principle. After the opening movements of the war, ending in the battle of Brentford and the establishment of the King's headquarters at Oxford, every western road leading out of London was either blocked or dominated by a Royalist garrison: the Southampton road at Farnham, or later at Winchester; the Exeter road by the garrison of Basing House; the Bristol road at Reading and subsequently at Newbury, and the Gloucester road, even after the Parliament's forces had taken Abingdon, by the garrison at Wallingford; while the Worcester road through Islip and Woodstock, and the alternative loop by Buckingham, were menaced by the King's headquarters at Oxford and the Earl of Northampton's at Banbury. The position had been brought about by merely military considerations, and was not at first intended as a threat to London's trade. The King issued more than one proclamation against pillage, and as late as March 1643 it was possible for certain cloth-merchants of London whose laden waggons had been seized by the Basing House garrison, to proceed to Oxford, lay a complaint, and secure the release of their property.[1] But the official policy of keeping open the ordinary channels of supply had already been to all intents and purposes defeated by lack of discipline and the urgent need of horses. The King held roughly those districts where packhorse traffic prevailed and where most of the heavy hauling was done by oxen. He could therefore count upon a supply of saddle-horses and sumpters fit for cavalry work, but was ill provided with heavy draught-horses for his artillery and baggage-trains. These were bred chiefly in the south-east counties and south-east midlands, especially in Leicestershire and Hertfordshire, which supplied London dealers with the horses then considered most suitable for coach-teams.[2]

It was partly in the hope of collecting horses of this type that Prince Rupert made his plundering foray into Northamptonshire in 1643, where 'he seized upon at least twelve hundred, taken most of them from the plough and cart, . . . held a fair, and sold divers horses as well as goods'.[3] Meanwhile a source of

[1] *H.M. Com. Cowper*, II, 332.

[2] Prothero. *English Farming Past and Present*, p. 137.

[3] N. Wallington. *Historical Notices*, II, 138; and see II, 263 for an account of 1000 horses captured in Leicester, June, 1645.

supply had been found in the carriers' teams. It was too much to expect of an ambitious cavalry officer, whose troop might be mounted on ancestors of the Cleveland bay, but whose baggage had to move at the snail's pace of the draught-ox, that he would be deterred by the proclamation from commandeering a carrier's string of hearty Suffolk punches or old English blacks. On the very day when the King raised his standard Lord Compton's troop pounced on the unfortunate William Whitaker, who was carrying a load of clothes for shipment to the forces in Ireland, 'disposed of the clothes among the soldiers, and carried away the waggon and horses to the undoing of the carrier'[1]—thus setting a ball rolling which nothing could stop. When the King at last issued his proclamation in June 1643 forbidding trade with London he did little more than sanction a state of affairs which already existed. London was already blockaded on the west, not very closely or systematically, it is true, but so far effectively that the western cloth trade had been brought almost to a standstill. The only route to London from the west that offered even a fair measure of safety in 1643–4 was the wide detour by Gloucester, Chipping Camden, Warwick and Newport Pagnel. This was the road taken by Waller after his defeat at Lansdowne,[2] and it seems to have been the line by which communications were maintained with the Parliamentary force besieged in Gloucester.

But the Gloucestershire clothiers who attempted this route with an escort of eighty men in the spring of 1645 had reason to regret it. 'The Earl of Northampton sent out a party of horse, about two hundred, from Banbury to wait for the Gloucestershire clothiers', and when they had intelligence of the clothiers coming they drew out after them and had a short skirmish, took about fifty prisoners, and all the cloth and horses. There was seventy two packs of cloth, which is valued at ten thousand pound'.[3] Such were the hazards of the easiest route. Farther south goods-traffic had become almost impossible except under strong escort. A convoy of eighty waggons from the west reached London safely on 17 June 1644; but in the same week we hear of two waggons and a string of pack-horses taken near

[1] Rushworth's *Collections*, Pt. iii, Vol. I, 777.
[2] J. Webb. *Memorials of the Civil War in Herefordshire*, I, 304.
[3] N. Wallington. *Historical Notices*, II, 256. Whitelocke. *Memorials*, p. 131.

Marlborough, and of sixteen waggons and forty pack-horses near Andover. Road-waggons are plundered near Marlborough again in the following January; the Chichester road-waggon is captured by the Basing garrison in July, and six cloth-waggons are plundered 'to the bare sticks' near Wallingford in October.[1] These are incidents that happen to be reported in the diurnals, because the loss involved was heavy. There must have been many less conspicuous cases of the same kind.

It is clear that the carriers still tried to maintain a regular service, but their difficulties were increased by traffic spies. One of these, Corporal Tobias Bazeley, was arrested in London in March 1645. Before the war he had been a porter for the Nottingham carriers at the Ram in Smithfield, and was employed by the garrison of Basing House partly as a bullet-moulder and partly as a traffic-spy. He was convicted of having 'betrayed divers carriers with their waggons too and carriages to the cavaliers', says *Mercurius Civicus*, and was hanged, 'full of imprecations', as a warning to others.

It is clear that under these war-time conditions to travel in large columns or companies had become the worst possible policy. It merely furnished the traffic-spy with something obvious to report, and concentrated in convenient shape the booty which a garrison was anxious to secure. Its commander might think twice about turning out a troop to capture a couple of carts; but to capture a whole column of transport was worth some risk and effort. Hence, instead of distributing their transport over a mile or two of road, it had become better policy for the carriers to distribute it over the days in the week. The garrison commander might choose his day, and make his raid, and somebody might have to suffer. But the action, as soon as it was reported, might be expected to draw troops from the nearest Parliamentary garrison into that sector, and the road would probably be safe enough for the rest of the week.

That the carriers had modified their plans in this direction is at least suggested by the second edition of Taylor's *Carrier's Cosmography*, which was published with a set of maps under the title of *A Brief director to the English Traveller* in 1645. It is in the main a careless reprint of the 1637 edition, repeating much detail that must have been out of date; but it gives some new

[1] G. N. Goodwin. *The Civil War in Hampshire.*

information, especially about the Chester road, which had never been actually blocked by the Royalists, but had been constantly harassed by troops of the notorious 'Rob-Carrier', Colonel Hastings, operating from Ashby-de-la-Zouch. The new information suggests how anxious the carriers were to avoid 'bunching' on this hazardous road. Thus a group of carriers from Bury, Rochdale, Colne, Wigan and Warrington come in on Wednesday; but the Kendal, Macclesfield, Congleton and Northwich men, who might have been expected to travel with them, prefer to let them pass and come in on Thursday. The carrier from Middlewich, which belongs geographically to the latter group, apparently thinks the road too crowded on that day, and elects to come in on Friday with the Chester carrier, who has changed his day from Thursday to Friday perhaps for the same reason; while the little Lancashire or Cheshire place called Bampton (?Barnton), apparently alarmed by the prospect of so much rich company in the latter part of the week, changes his day from Thursday to Tuesday, and has the road to himself. The evidence is slender, and taken from a pamphlet so carelessly printed as the *Brief director* must be accepted with caution; but for what it may be worth, it does suggest that the carriers were modifying their system of travel to meet the special problems created by the war. The underlying principle remained the same. It consisted of presenting, as far as possible, a scattered target, so that if one individual or group became a casualty, the others would probably escape.

The advantage of this principle, whether in peace or war, is obvious: members of the public gained by it a higher average of security for their goods in transit. But it is to be noted that in peace time they paid for it in opportunities of sending and receiving. A shop-keeper in such a place as Towcester, situated on a busy high-road, might be able to count a dozen London waggons passing his door in the course of the week; but under this system they might all pass on the same day. His opportunities of replenishing his stock or executing London orders might therefore be no more frequent than they would have been in a remote country place served by a village higgler.

How far this was a handicap depended upon the nature of his business. The provincial mercer or haberdasher tried to overcome the difficulty by laying in a more varied stock than his successor in the age of railways. Indeed, it is rather surprising to note, in the inventories published by the Surtees society, what choice and expensive cloth, for instance, might be bought in what was evidently a tiny village shop. The stock of such wares is, of course, small; but it shows that a provincial shopkeeper could count upon a certain amount of 'high class' trade with the gentry in his neighbourhood. Thus Lord Howard of Naworth has his breeches and jerkin made in Penrith, and his lady buys there the ribbons, rebato wires, silk buttons, silver lace and herring-bone lace required for her new gown, as well as the materials for her children's clothes. The Penrith mercer would hardly have had this custom if there had been readier access to the London shops, and he would probably have said that so far from losing by a defective transport system his business gained by it. But any trade which depended upon quick and frequent access to its source of supply must have been at a great disadvantage, and the most obvious example is bookselling.

There is perhaps no trade in which it is more important to satisfy the customer's demand promptly than bookselling, because there is none in which the demand itself is so particular and so perishable. A man who asks for salmon may be willing to buy trout, and the lady who has had thoughts of velvet may be tempted to paduasoy. But the young amorist who asks for *The Academy of Compliments* cannot be fobbed off with *Baxter on Grace*, and the lady who wants Mrs. Manly's *New Atalantis* cannot be persuaded to mean the well known work by Lord Verulam. Moreover, unless the demand is met promptly it may evaporate. It is quite unsafe to assume that the young gentleman will want the same book in a month's time. He may have borrowed it; or he may have married the girl; or she may have jilted him and left him unfit for anything but *A Few Signs from Hell*. The difficulty, for a bookseller, of keeping abreast with the varied and fleeting demands of his clients is great even now, and in the seventeenth century it was almost insuperable. Until the disorganization brought about by the Civil War the only printing presses licensed in England were in London, York and the two University towns. Every English-printed book sold by a law-abiding country bookseller had to be fetched from one of those places, and had to be sold at an enhanced price to cover the carriage and his profit. Unless he was a freeman of the Stationers' Company and could get some of his stock on trade terms, his profit was bound to be small. Old James Cock, the mercer of Kendal who supplied Sir Daniel Fleming with books, used to present his account under three heads: so much for the book at the London price; so much for carriage; and so much for what he blithely calls 'profit'. On eight separate transactions between March and September 1669, involving some fifty items, his total 'profit' amounted to *5s.* 10*d.*[1] Evidently then, since the profits were small it was very desirable that there should be 'quick returns'. But the carrier took eighteen days coming and going between London and Chester in 1635; three weeks between London and Prescott (near Liverpool) in 1630; about a month between London and Barnstaple in 1617; and probably five weeks between London and Kendal at the time of Sir Daniel's purchases. As for Scotland and Ireland, 'if anie of his Majesty's subjects shall write to Madrill in Spaine', says Thomas Witherings in 1635, 'hee shall receive answer sooner and surer than hee shall out of Scotland or Ireland. The letters being now carried by carriers or footposts 16 or 18 miles a day, it is full two monethes before any answer can be received from Scotland or Ireland to London'.

It is therefore not surprising that provincial bookselling developed slowly and was nearly always a side line carried by a shop dealing in other merchandise. Only eleven provincial towns (other than Oxford, Cambridge and York) are known to have had a bookseller before 1600; only eighteen between 1601 and 1641, and only thirty-four between 1641 and 1667. There seems to be no record of a bookseller in Bristol before 1620, in Manchester before 1633, in Carlisle before 1656, or in Leicester before 1661. Important towns like Bedford, Reading and Chippenham apparently had no bookseller until the reign of Queen Anne.[2]

This was due primarily, no doubt, to the small size of the provincial reading public, which in many places was too widely scattered to provide a trade except for the travelling book pedlar; but the slow rhythm of communications must have added

[1] J. McGrath. *The Flemings at Oxford,* Vol. I, Appendix E.

[2] J. McKerrow. *A Dictionary of Printers and Booksellers,* 1557–1640. R. C. Plomer (ditto), 1641–67 and 1668–1725.

greatly to the country bookseller's difficulties. It was all very well for people like Lady Harley to say 'the shureness of the carrier, tho he is slow, makes me writ by him'; or for young Anthony Gawdy to compare him to the hedgehog in the fable—'I have heard that the hedgehogg overcame the hare; and so the carryer may overrun the post'.[1] These fine ladies and gentlemen were not trying to scrape a living by selling books in some little one-horse town at the end of a long muddy road.

[1] *H.M. Com. 7th Report*, Appendix, p. 520.

VIII

Footposts

ONE reason for the slowness of the carrier's rhythm was that he often had to wait a day or two in Town for his return lading. 'A carrier sets out from Westchester to London on the Monday, which is 120 miles', says Witherings, the new Postmaster, in 1635. 'The said carrier is eight days upon the road, and upon his coming to London, delivers letters of advice for his reloading to Westchester again, and is forced to stay in London two days, at extraordinary charges, before he can get his reloading ready. By this conveyance (i.e. the Post) letters will be from Westchester to London in one day and night, so that the said carrier's loading will be ready a week before the said carriers shall come to London; and they no sooner come to London, but may be ready to depart again'.[1]

This promised to remove a handicap which the carriers had tried for many years to overcome, or at least to reduce, by the use of footposts.

The prestige of the footpost, which stood high in the seventeenth century, depended on the fact that the average speed of a horse falls off much more steeply than that of a man as the distance is increased. Over a few miles a horse may go at twenty-five miles an hour. When Henrietta Maria landed at Dover in June 1625, Robert Tyrwhitt, who carried the news to the King at

[1] *A Proposition for the Settling of Staffets or pacquet posts*, 1635. As printed in the *Report* of the Secret Committee on the Post Office, 1844.

Canterbury, did the fifteen miles in thirty-six minutes.[1] But the conspirator Rookwood, compelled to ride double that distance without change of horse on his desperate flight to Ashby St. Leger, could not do better than fifteen miles an hour,[2] and it was found (or firmly believed) that over long journeys of several days' duration a horse was actually not as fast as a well trained man on foot. The foot guides supplied to Thomas Kirk at Dundee in 1677 would 'undertake to run down the best horse you can buy in seven or eight days',[3] and Sir William Petty, in his plan for raising the speed of the postal service to five miles an hour thought that 'it may better be performed by men exercised in it, by reason footmen can go where horses cannot'.[4]

Unless relays of horses could be established, therefore, the quickest means of communication over long distances was believed to be by running footmen, and these had become an indispensable part of a Tudor gentleman's establishment. The best of them were Irish kernes: tough, rangy fellows like the men of Tyrone's bodyguard who, says Spenser, 'in the frost wade as familiarly as water spaniels'. It was noted that, unlike the English, they thought 'a low pitcht Calf the best Leg, and therefore they stroak down the Calfs of their Legs; a high great bellied Leg, it may be, being found somewhat inconvenient in running of long Races'.[5] 'Many of them', says Ludovico in *The Honest Whore*, become 'footmen to noblemen and others; and the knaves are very faithful where they love. By my faith, very proper men, many of them, and as active as the clouds—whirrh ha!' They were encouraged to keep their kerne's 'glibbe', 'a thicke curled bush of hair hanging down over their eyes'. It was thought ornamental ('for man shews more venerable', says Bulwer, 'if his hairs be fairly superaboundantly circumfused'), and it could even on occasion be useful.

A secret letter could be sent 'wrapped in the long hair of an Irish laquey' with every confidence that it would escape

[1] *Finetti Philoxenis*, 1656, p. 153.

[2] Tristram. *Coaching Days*, 1924, p. 339.

[3] *An Account of a Tour in Scotland by Thomas Kirk*, ed. Hume Brown, 1892, p. 20.

[4] *The Petty Papers*, ed. The Marquis of Lansdowne, 1927, II, 203.

[5] R. Bulwer. *Anthropometamorphosis*, 1650, p. 235; Dekker. *The Honest Whore* (2), I, 1.

search.[1] That they were popularly associated with secret service of this kind is quaintly revealed by the dramatic 'reporter' who, trying to recall the Queen's speech in *Henry VI* (*Part 2*):–

> I will repeale thee, or be well assured
> Adventure to be banished myself,

produced instead:

> Ile have an Irish that shall find thee out,
> And long thou shalt not stay, but Ile have thee repelde.

It was a plausible addition, for an Irish footman was thought capable of finding anything, 'tho' 'twere hidden under a mine of sea cole'.

His normal duty, as servant to an English nobleman, was 'to runne bare-headed by his horse bellie', receiving a new pair of shoes when they reached the outskirts of the city, and a special fuel-allowance or 'drying money' when they got in.[2] But this was mere routine. 'How farre canst runne in a daie?' asks the King in *The Welsh Ambassador*. 'My faat' replies Teage, 'I salbee loate to have dine horse runne so farre in a daie as I can'. A footman named Laughan, in the service of Lord Berkeley, 'upon the sickness of the Lady Katherine, this Lord's wife, carried a letter from Callowden to old Doctor Fryer, a physician then dwelling in Little Britain, in London, and returned with a glass bottle in his hand compounded by the Doctor for recovery of her health; a journey of 148 miles performed by him in less than 42 hours, (notwithstanding his stay over one night at the physician and apothecary's house), which no one horse could have so well and safely performed; for which the lady shortly after gave him a new suite of clothes'.[3]

The choice of shock-headed Irishmen for this service was, no doubt, dictated partly by fashion, and the fine lady in *The Soddered Citizen* who insists that her laqueys shall not be 'dull Country footpost fellows, but swiftest Irishe', is thinking chiefly of appearances. But that able-bodied runners were regarded as a practical necessity is seen in the fact that they were regularly employed by many Towns and Corporations to carry their

[1] Sadler. II, 449.

[2] *The Welsh Ambassador* (Malone Soc.), line 1163; *The Puritane Widow*, I, 4, 218; *The Soddered Citizen* (Malone Soc.), line 722. And see Note 09.

[3] J. Smyth. *Lives of the Berkeleys*, 1883, II, 381; and see Note 010.

official correspondence. The footpost of Bristol, Thomas Lyne (who was also, from 1532 to 1591, 'Bedel of the Rogues', and evidently a tough fellow), regularly travelled between Bristol and London with letters to and from the Lord Treasurer, receiving on each occasion 13*s.* 4*d.*, or occasionally 15*s.*, for the return journey of 240 miles.

He may have made something extra for himself by carrying private letters as well, but 15*s.* was his official maximum; and it was evidently thought sufficient, for when, on one occasion, the Lord Treasurer gave him 4*s.* 6*d.* as 'portage' on two unofficial letters, the sum was thriftily deducted from his allowance by the Bristol chamberlain.[1] Similar footposts were employed by many other towns. In 1654 one Bartholamew Moore complains that he has 'for five years performed the hard and toilsome service of footpost from Leicester to London, and thence to Leicester again every week, being more than ever yet was done by any man in England, and during all the said five years your Petitioner never miscarried in his journies and returns above three or four times'.[2] If his claim was true he must have done 204 miles a week and, unless he travelled on Sunday, must have kept up an average of thirty-four miles a day: about twice the rate of an ordinary carrier. There were also cruising footposts, like the rascal described in *The Life of Gamaliel Ratsey* (1605), who went 'with a long pikt staffe on his neck and a leatherne bag overthwart his shoulder and under his arm', and when asked where he was going, would reply gaily 'Faith, I go every way, even as the directions of my letters give me occasion'.

Some of these men were prepared to carry heavy goods. In 1625 Valentine Pettit sends seventeen yards of damask and other London purchases to his sister at Barham 'by Gybbson, the foote post of Canterbury', and Edmund Verney sends his bedding home from Winchester 'by the footepost which goeth from Winchester to Oxford'.[3] For such jobs they must have used horses, and become indistinguishable from ordinary carriers. But they retained their title of 'footpost' for a particular reason.

In 1635, by the patent granted to Thomas Witherings, the

[1] *Mayor's Audits*, in the Bristol Archives.

[2] M. Bateson. *Records of the Borough of Leicester*, IV, 423

[3] *The Oxinden Letters*, ed. Gardiner, 1923, I, 25; *Memoirs of the Verney Family*, 1907, I, 99.

conveyance of private letters at posting speed was made the monopoly of the Government posts. This was ignored by the eastern clothiers, who had long been in the habit of sending a mounted man ahead of their carts with business letters and orders. In 1637 therefore Jason Grover (variously described as 'post' and 'carrier' of Ipswich) was arrested and charged with infringing the patent, and the matter came before the Privy Council. Their decision was embodied in a proclamation of 1638:

> Common known carriers . . . are hereby permitted to carry any letters along with their carts, waggons or pack-horses, travelling with the same the ordinary known journeys that common carriers use to travel.
> PROVIDED always that they, or any of their servants, at no time stay at any place from whence they carry any letters above eight hours after their carts, waggons or pack-horses are departed, nor bring any letters to London, or elsewhere, above eight hours before the said carts, waggons or pack-horses shall come there.

In effect this meant that all cruising footposts were to be suppressed, and that the men on established beats were not to go above a footman's pace. It was therefore worth a footpost's while to retain his old title, even if he had become indistinguishable from an ordinary carrier, since it advertised his compliance with this order, and made it clear that although he was prepared to carry letters, he had no intention of invading the Government post's monopoly of *grande vitesse*.

It was not until 1663, when the farm of the Post Office had been granted to Daniel O'Neale, that a proclamation was issued forbidding all persons whatsoever except Daniel O'Neale or his deputies 'to carry or deliver letters for hire'.[1] But the machinery of the Government Post was still so small that the order could not be effectively enforced. Footposts were still necessary in many districts which the horse-post did not touch, and the habit of sending letters by the carrier was so well established that O'Neale professed that he would rather resign his post than go to the trouble of proceding against every offender. Unofficial footposts therefore survived in some places even until the nineteenth century. A woman called Mally Messenger (probably an occupative name) who died in Keswick in 1856 at the age of

[1] Hyde. p. 271.

93, had on several occasions in her youth walked to London and back. She used to boast that on one of her journeys a Keswick man on horseback, who overtook her coming out of London, shouted as he passed 'I'll tell them in Keswick you're coming', and that she got to Keswick before him.[1] She was making the traditional claim of the footpost to have gone faster than a horse.

How fast these footposts really went it is difficult to say. They can have had no difficulty in outpacing the waggon traffic of the south and east, but whether they did much better time than the northern pack-trains is more doubtful. In practice their pace did not much matter. Their usefulness depended on the fact that they could be sent off a few days ahead of the carrier's gang with letters and orders for his return loading, thus simplifying his business and expediting his 'turn round'. In this way they indubitably did something to mitigate the slowness of communications. But not very much. As long as the carrier was primarily a goods-haulier, the speed with which he and his passengers could move was necessarily restricted to the speed at which heavy goods could be shifted along execrable roads. It was only if he could get rid of his heavy goods and concentrate upon his passengers—only if he could turn hackneyman outright—that he would be able to offer a more rapid service.

[1] D. Scott. *Bygone Cumberland and Westmoreland*, 1899, p. 210.

IX

Horse Relays and Standing Posts

THE slowness of the carrier was accepted as inevitable, and at ordinary times the public was content to let its affairs move at the carrier's pace. But there were occasions when it was absolutely necessary to travel, or send a message, faster than any single horse or footpost could run, and when therefore relays of horses had to be used. Robert Aske, the leader of the Pilgrimage of Grace, on being summoned to London in 1536 laid private relays at Ware, Huntingdon and Lincoln, in order that, if he were arrested, news might be sent at once to his adherents; Sir Peter Carew prepared to join the Wyatt rebellion by laying posthorses 'by all London way to Andover and elsewhere'; the Gunpowder Plotters had their relays between London and Dunchurch; and Sir Robert Cary, in anticipation of Queen Elizabeth's death, had evidently laid private stages all the way to Edinburgh, in order that he might be the first to hail her successor.[1] There was nothing to prevent any private person from making such arrangements if he thought them worth the expense.

But the expense was serious. The Bristol footpost, as we have seen, could travel to London and back for 15*s*. If he had been sent in post (at a time when Government stages were available

[1] Froude's *History*, III, 595; *Life and Times of Sir Peter Carew*, ed. Maclean, 1857, p. 179; *Correspondence of James VI* (Camd. Soc.), p. 49. There were no regular post-stages north of Berwick until after the Queen's death.

on that road) his travelling expenses would have been 74*s.*—quite enough to frighten a city chamberlain. But if the corporation had been obliged for some reason to establish and equip these stages with men and horses of their own, I calculate that at 3*s.* 4*d.* a day (their usual allowance to a mounted messenger), the cost of establishing, using, and subsequently withdrawing the relays would have been something like £8. It need hardly be said that correspondence at this rate was quite beyond the ordinary citizen, and could be contemplated only by very rich or very anxious gentlemen.

But there was one gentleman in Tudor England who was in a position to manage it more cheaply. The king enjoyed the prerogative of 'purveyance': an ancient and customary right of spoil which enabled him not only to demand the use of his subjects' goods, but to pay for them at a rate fixed (in practice) by his own assessors. It was therefore unnecessary for him to send out his own horses and men to serve along the route which his dispatches were to travel. Instead he (or the Council on his behalf) simply provided the messenger himself with an 'open placart', requiring all public officers instantly, and at their utmost peril, to 'take up' horses for his use at the King's price of one penny a mile. This document created a state of emergency in any town where it was presented, and the duties which it imposed were exactly the same as if a relay of horses had previously been laid there. It was in fact a command that a relay should be improvised; and its effect was that the relays between London and Bristol which would have cost any private person £8 to establish, could be improvised and used by the King for just 40*s.* 2*d.*

Now if 'open placarts' had created a mechanism usable by the public, there would probably have been little complaint, although a penny a mile was less than half the usual rate of hire; for the inhabitants of coastal and border districts (to name no others) had a personal as well as a national interest in the maintenance of rapid communications, and any system that would have enabled them not merely to receive but also to send a message quickly in times of danger would have been well worth paying for. But the 'open placart' system created nothing. As soon as the messenger had passed normal stagnation was restored, and the town was as far from help in an emergency as ever. The 'open placart' enabled the King, so to speak, to 'ring up' the Mayor of Plymouth. But the Mayor of Plymouth could not 'ring up' the King. His expensive telephone had earphones but no mouthpiece, and the speed with which he could summon assistance in an emergency depended still upon the good will of his neighbours and the public alarm that events might have aroused. Panic might help his messenger to fresh horses along a threatened seaboard and through the country next adjoining, but even the liveliest panic soon lost its momentum further inland. A post letter of 1599 announcing (mistakenly) that the Spanish fleet was preparing to assault Plymouth in full force, travelled from Exeter to Honiton at eight miles an hour, from Honiton to Crewkerne at eight, from Crewkerne to Sherborne at seven, from Sherborne to Shaftesbury at five, and from Shaftesbury to Salisbury and thence to Andover at less than three. So remote seemed the Spanish menace in the green vastness of Salisbury plain.[1]

It is only natural, therefore, that 'open placarts' should have been unpopular, and for that reason they tended to become ineffective at times of crisis when they were most necessary. As long as the royal dispatches were few and far between the King's messenger, pouncing unexpectedly on some country town, could be pretty sure of finding a tolerable horse. But as soon as some public crisis made it probable that Government couriers would be passing thick and fast along a particular road, it became a matter of common prudence for horse owners thereabouts to remove their best geldings to a distance, in order to save them from being worked to death at the King's beggarly price.

As early as 1392 we find a certain Henry Draper under arrest at Northampton because, when the King's messengers were coming through the town, 'he withdrew himself and his horses, delaying the King's business in contempt of the King',[2] and we may be sure that such incidents were common. They were bound to occur as long as the King's price was uneconomic and no compensatory advantage was secured by the public. Elizabeth's government, prompted by her very intelligent Postmaster

[1] *Lieutenant Edward Doddington to the Privy Council*, 25 July 1599, S.P.12. CCLXI. 115.

[2] *Calendar of Close Rolls* 1392–6, p. 9.

Sir Thomas Randolph, soon recognized this fact, and in times of stress (e.g. during the northern rebellion of 1569) doubled the Queen's price; but in the fifteenth century the remedy adopted seems to have been simply to increase the number of purveyors authorized to take up horses by royal warrant. Some of the numerous patentees whose names appear in the *Calendar of Patent Rolls* were no doubt responsible officers who used their powers with discretion, but it had become the practice to sell commissions of this kind to speculators who, as might have been expected, used them as a means of extorting money from horse owners. The preamble of an Act of 1449 states that

> divers Hostlers, Brewers and other Victuallers have purchased the King's Letters Patents to take Horses and Carts for the carriage of the King and Queen, . . . by colour of which they daily take Horses and Carts where no need is, and bring them to the Hosteries, and there keep them secretly, some time until they have spent XXd or XLd of their Stuff; and then they make the Owners to pay for the same before they can get delivery of their Horses and Carts, and some till they have made a Fine with them; . . . and of some the King's People they take Fines to shew favour and not to take their Horses and Carts; so that divers Persons be greatly endamaged by the said Takers, as well for the non payment of the Hire of the said Horses . . . as for the great charge they have for their meat, and Fines made for their delivery.

The Act is an attempt to stop this racket by declaring all such patents void and enacting that no horse shall be taken 'but by the Delivery of the Mayor, Sheriff, Bailiff or Constable'. But this merely reasserts an old rule of purveyance dating from the time of Edward III, and it leaves the real problem untouched. The fundamental difficulty was that the affairs of Government now needed a better system of communications than the old courier service, based on requisitioned horses, could supply. For at his brightest and best the courier was no better than the hare in the fable. However peremptory his placart, and however promptly he might be served with horses, he could not continue to ride them indefinitely without intervals for food and sleep. Over long distances, therefore, he could not hope to compete with a mechanism of standing posts, by which letters could be passed from hand to hand and thus travel steadily, though perhaps at a slower pace, by night as well as day. It was no doubt the inefficiency of the old courier service, as well as its great unpopularity, that prompted Henry VIII in 1511 to appoint Brian Tuke 'Master of the Posts',[1] with authority to establish a certain number of 'standing Posts in pay'.

It was still an exercise of the royal prerogative of purveyance, and the responsibility for forwarding the King's dispatches still rested upon the local authorities. Instead of 'hable and sufficient horses' they were now to provide 'an able man well horsed'. The difference was that the King was now prepared to assist his subjects in the performance of this duty by paying wages to the man whom they selected to serve. The payment was therefore a kind of subsidy, or the part-remission of a tax, and it was entirely subject to the King's pleasure. It was liable to be suspended at any moment in favour of the old system, and many populous districts never benefited by it at all. But while and where 'standing posts' were in pay they turned what was essentially a royal exaction into something like a public benefit. When horses had to be 'taken up', as was still very often the case, it was a great relief to busy mayors and bailiffs to have on the spot an official responsible for taking them; and the privilege of being able (with due pretext and warrant) to whizz up to London at a speed of, perhaps, seven miles an hour opened a new chapter in our social history. It was, of course, in no sense a new invention. On the Continent a vast organization of posts and couriers had been established and extended throughout the Emperor's dominions from 1491 onwards by the Counts von Thurn und Taxis, and when Brian Tuke sat down to draw up orders for his posts he must have had this great system in mind.[2] But the English posting arrangements were not a mere copy or extension of the Continental. More than a century before the first Count von Taxis received his patent a small but vigorous posting system had been worked out on the Dover road by the enterprising hackneymen of Kent, and it was upon this native stock that the Tudor Post was grafted.

[1] His patent has not been found, and seems never to have been properly recorded, since in 1545 the Privy Council had to ask his son to return the original to assist them in drafting the patent for his successor (Dasent I, 267). The first recorded payment to Tuke as Master of the Posts was made in Feb. 1512.

L.P.F.D. *Henry VIII.*
Vol. II, Pt. 2, 1454.

[2] J. Rubsam. *Early Posts of the Tyrol*, printed in *Union Postale*, XVI, 197.

X

The Kentish Stages

'SIR, ye know well', writes Tuke to Cromwell in 1533, 'that except the hakney horses bitwene Gravesende and Dovour, there is no such usual conveyance in post for men in this realme as in the accustomed places of France and other parties'.[1] It is clear from this that the only road in England over which the volume of passenger traffic had been large and steady enough to provide work for a system of regular hackney stages was the old pilgrim way to Canterbury and the port of Dover.

A patent of 1396 makes it clear that at some time before that date the road had been organized in stages, and that the fare per stage (presumably for official riders or couriers) had been fixed at 1*s.* 4*d.* This had proved to be more than the couriers were willing to pay, and the hackneymen, through their spokesmen, Reginald Shrewsbury and Thomas Athecok, complained that 'divers men passing through these parts take the horses against their will, paying little or nothing', and that they are often 'lost or sold or taken quite away'. The King therefore ordains by this patent that

> there shall be taken for the hire of a hakenei from Suthwerk to Rocester 12d, from Roucester to Canterbury 12d, and from Canterbury to Dover 6d, and from town to town according to the rate of 12d and the number of the miles; that the petitioners be in nonwise compelled to let their horses for hire unless paid promptly; and

[1] Brian Tuke to Cromwell, 17 Aug. 1533.

> that for the better security of the horses a branding-iron be kept in each of those towns by an approved person for branding, without payment, horses on hire.[1]

How long before 1396 these stages had been in operation is not indicated, but the fact that Chaucer in his *Prologue* written only a few years earlier, mentions no hackneys, branded or unbranded, may warrant the guess that they were a recent development. They had been in existence long enough, however, for over-thrifty travellers to discover a method of bilking the hackneymen by pretending to be royal messengers and getting their horses at the couriers' rate. An Act of the next year (1397), though it does not specifically mention the hackneymen, recapitulates the abuses of which they had complained, and threatens with imprisonment 'People of evill Condition which, of their own Authority take and cause to be taken royally Horses and other things, . . . saying and devising that they be to ride on hasty Messages and Business, where of Truth they be in no wise privy to any Business or Message'.

Whether the hackneymen had anticipated the methods of the Tudor Post by passing the royal packet from hand to hand there is nothing to show. But it is very improbable. For many years after the royal post was instituted, this new-fangled way of handling the King's letters seemed to the older officials dangerous and indecent. It was an indecorum which they would never have tolerated in their correspondence with each other. A gentleman's letter was always to be carried by a servant or personal representative, and presented with proper ceremony. That had always been the courtly rule. And now, to have a thumbed and grimy packet thrust into one's hand, scrawled over with illiterate endorsements and decorated, as likely as not, with a crude sketch of the gallows for the intimidation of post-boys —it was more than a gentleman of the old school could stomach.

'What my Lord Lieutenant means I know not', wrote Mr. Uvedale hotly, upon receiving such a packet from Lord Grey in 1548, 'or whether he means it towards the posts; but it is a token for murderers and thieves, and not for so true a man and old a servant as I'.[2] It was a long time before the Postmaster could persuade old-fashioned officials of this type to send their

[1] *C.P.R.* 1396.
[2] *C.S.P.Dom.* (Addenda 1548), p. 383.

letters by post instead of by expensive couriers, and even up to the end of Elizabeth's reign whenever reports were to be sent to the Queen by the ordinary post, definite instructions had to be issued to that effect. The mere effluvium of a postal packet was supposed to be too much for her on ordinary occasions: a fact of which her Secretary is said once to have taken advantage when 'a Post from Scotland meeting her Majesty upon Greenwich Heath, Sir Robert Cecil would needs cut open the packet, and pretending it stunk, had time to perfume it, and convey away his own letters'.[1]

It is therefore highly improbable that in 1396 the Kentish hackneymen were already handling the royal dispatches. Their official duty was almost certainly confined to supplying horses for the couriers who rode through with them. But their system of stages was an important service to the public, and soon became so efficient that it was highly praised by foreign visitors to England. Paul Hentzner, who posted from Rye to London in 1598, at a time when there were no Government stages on that road, was astonished at the speed of the horses which the hackneymen supplied. 'It is surprising how swiftly they run', he says, 'their bridles are very light, and their saddles little more than a span over'.[2] It is true that among Englishmen they were the target of many jokes, and 'a Rochester hackney' was often mentioned as an epitome of all the ills that horse-flesh is heir to. He was 'a dreaming dromedary'.[3] He would 'stumble three hours in one mile; . . . if one ran him he would simper and mump, as though he had gone awooing to a maltmare at Rochester'.[4] But Englishmen of that time were notoriously hard riders: 'they ride', says James Howell, 'as if they rid for a midwife, or a Physician, or to get a Pardon to save one's life, as he goeth to execution';[5] and they had already developed that curious snobbery about horses which used to make so much matter for *Punch*. In fact the 'false gallop after some ten miles an hour,' with which Fynes Moryson credits the English post-horses,

[1] Lloyd's *Statesmen and Favourites*, 1665, p. 508.

[2] *Itinerary*, III, 479. There had been post-stages at Chipstead, Flimwell and Rye between September 1589 and March 1590, but at no other time in the sixteenth century.

[3] From *Whimsies or a New Cast of Characters*, 1631 (A Postmaster).

[4] John Lyly. *Mother Bombie*, IV, ii, 206.

[5] *Instructions for Forreine Travel*, ed. Arber, p. 69.

came to be called 'a Canterbury gallop', and has left us the English word 'canter': surely a respectable legacy, more convincing than all the jokes.

But the best evidence that the Kentish posting system was a flourishing concern is the fact that when the royal post was instituted in 1511 the hackneymen of the Dover road were found to be so well intrenched in their privileges that their customs had to be allowed for in the new regulations.

On all other roads the traveller paid by the mile, but on the Dover road he paid half a crown a stage, which at reputed mileage worked out at a penny a mile more than the rate allowed elsewhere. The posts of the other roads were 'posts in pay', receiving (after 1557) a standard daily wage of 1*s.* 8*d.*; but until 1589 those on the Dover road were simply selected hackneymen who contracted to forward the royal Packet at a charge of 1*s.* 8*d.* a stage; and they continued to serve on this basis until the growth of official correspondence made it more costly than day-wages. The post of Rochester, for instance, claimed and received payment in 1564 for 79 packets, in 1576 for 135, in 1581 for 172, in 1586 for 275, in 1588 for 349, and in 1589 for 392.[1] At that date, therefore, his remuneration at 1*s.* 8*d.* a packet had become more costly to the Queen than wages at 1*s.* 8*d.* a day.

The Government got over the difficulty by suddenly appointing all the men on this road 'extraordinary posts', and according to the invariable practice when such posts had to be appointed for a progress or other special occasion, putting them on day-wages. They continue to appear in the accounts as 'extraordinary posts' until 1594, when the device is dropped, and they are described as 'ordinary Posts . . . heretofore accustomed to be paid by the packet, but now reduced to a certain rate'. The old custom of payment by the stage lasted until 1603. Thus in the end the Kentish hackneymen and their stages were merged in the royal posting system, having been in fact the stock upon which it was grafted. But they never took kindly to it. One of the old rules of the Dover road had been that 'no hackneyman shall break another's hire',[2] and this granting of special privileges to certain of their members, with exclusive use of 'guide

[1] *P.O. Accounts.*
[2] *H.M. Com. Rochester*, p. 287.

and horn', seemed to them an invasion of their traditional liberties. They persisted in flouting the regulations, and furnishing travellers with 'guide and horn' in spite of all that the Postmaster could do. 'As the case now standeth', says Randolph, upon taking over the Postmaster's duties in 1566, 'every hackneyman taketh upon him the Queen's standing post, especially when any gain is offered'.[1] Even as late as 1609 the *Orders* for Kent are still concerned with the 'disorders offered by certain persons called hackneymen, tapsters, hostlers and others, in hiring out their horses to the hindrance of public service, danger to our State, and wrong to our standing and settled Posts in their several stages'.

As this Order indicates, one of the reasons why the Government was anxious to impose discipline upon the hackneymen of Kent was that their horses were so readily available to foreign spies and agents. The enigmatic stranger, usually described as 'like a seminary priest', who was from time to time reported to have landed at some quiet Kentish port, taken horse from an obliging hackneyman, and vanished down a side-road, was the cause of much official headache. A special order of 1584 therefore provided that in Kent 'all strangers, whether they ride in post or by journey, shall take their horses from stage to stage, and at the hands of the standing Posts only, or with their knowledge and appointment'. The stranger's particulars were to be entered in the post's ledger at each stage as he passed on his way. If he tried to diverge from the post-road, he was to be detained 'till notice be given either to her Majesty's Secretary or the Master of the Posts', and might find himself proceeding to London under an armed escort, in charge of the post whom he had tried to evade. The purpose was to ensure that the foreign visitor who landed at Dover, Sandwich or Margate should ride straight forward to London before proceeding to any other destination. And this no doubt is what usually happened. But a good deal depended upon the individual hackneyman's respect for the Postmaster and his regulations. It was not usually whole-hearted, and there is little doubt that a man who required horses for some secret errand, and was prepared to pay well for them, could always get them in Elizabethan Kent.

[1] *Reasons to move her Majesty . . . for the redress of many things concerning the Posts,* 1566. S.P. 12, XLI, 71.

XI

Monopoly by Bargain

THE Dover road had special privileges and presented special problems for the Postmaster; but on all the other roads a post was regarded, for administrative purposes, simply as a Messenger of the Chamber on permanent riding duty, and at first was paid no more than a Messenger's usual riding allowance of 12*d.* a day. For this he was required to carry the royal Packet over the ten or fifteen miles of his stage at any hour of the day or night: a duty obviously demanding the use of more than one horse. But it was admitted by the Postmaster himself that a man could hardly be expected to keep more than one horse available for the purpose for such a small wage.[1] One of the first problems confronting the Postmaster, therefore, was how to induce the posts to keep more horses without doubling or trebling their wages; and the expedient adopted, perhaps in Henry VIII's reign and certainly before the end of Queen Mary's, was to strike a tacit bargain with the authorities of the post towns. The towns were still responsible, as has been said, for furnishing horses at a penny a mile on demand. It was a great nuisance, and might become a serious burden, since a penny a mile was not an economic rate of hire. The inhabitants of Grantham, for instance, complained in 1578 that although they had no pasture in common, and were for the most part industrial

[1] Brian Tuke to Cromwell, 17 Aug. 1533. Printed in the *Report* of the Secret Committee on the Post Office 1844, p. 32.

workers, they had been required during the previous twelve months to find no less than 473 horses at a penny a mile, in addition to those provided by the post. Another town mentioned, but not named, by the Postmaster in 1583, had had to find a thousand.[1] But the position of such towns on busy main roads ensured them a certain amount of private passenger traffic which was prepared to pay twopence or twopence halfpenny a mile for the privilege of travelling fast. What the Government therefore in effect proposed was to make the post primarily responsible for the penny-a-mile work if, in return, the town would guarantee him first pick of the more lucrative traffic. The matter was never, I believe, put in terms of a bargain; but a bargain was implicit, and it offered an attractive solution for all concerned. Town authorities would be relieved of the odious job of 'taking up' horses, except when a large number should happen to be required; the post might be expected to prosper, and to keep more horses available, and—a very important point—private horse-owners would be entitled to refuse the use of their horses as long as the post had a horse standing in his stable. Nobody could have been expected to keep a horse for the penny-a-mile work without some compensatory advantage, for even if it could have been worked 100 miles a week, it is to be remembered that only about half of these miles would have been paid for, since after running its stage it would normally have been brought back riderless by the post-boy. Thus at a penny a mile the most that it would have been likely to earn was 4*s.* 2*d.*; and if Robert Loder's farm accounts are any guide, the horse would have had to earn at least 4*s.* 7*d.* a week to cover its own keep and that of the necessary post-boy.[2]

But with a guaranteed first call on the more lucrative traffic the post would be able to keep other horses which might bring him in eight or nine shillings each every week, thus making good his deficit on the penny-a-mile work, and leaving him with a margin of profit on his stable as a whole.

It was upon a basis of such calculations that the posting system was financed and regulated from the time of Queen Mary until the end of Elizabeth's reign. 'Whensoever any running

[1] *Petition of the Inhabitants of Grantham*, S.P. 12, CXXVII, 65. Randolph to Walsingham. S.P. 12, CLXIII, 76.

[2] See Note 011.

the post', say the draft *Orders* of 1575 'shall bring with them a commission for the taking up of horses', (i.e. at the Queen's price of a penny a mile), 'the same commission shall be first sent from the head Officer of the place to the ordinary Post, to thintent he may furnish the same with his horses, if he have so many. If he have not sufficient to serve the turn, then the said head Officers to assist him, for the furnishing of all such as shall lack, amongst those that use to hire horses, or elsewhere'. On the other hand if a private traveller applied for post-horses to a hackneyman (offering a lucrative rate of hire), 'the said hackneyman shall first bring the party desirous to ride in post unto the Post to be first served of him if he may, or otherwise to be furnished at his appointment, the Post withal taking his name'.

The monopoly thus secured for the posts extended only to rapid passenger traffic, riding from stage to stage.

'It is not intended hereby', say the *Orders* for Kent 1584, 'to hinder the liberty of any Englishman or natural born subject of this Realm riding in journey, but that he or they may take choice, and at such prices as they can. Provided that they ride not with horn nor guide, which marks are only reserved for the Posts to use or allow of, for the more safety in riding and better expedition'.

But the 'journey' rate for the ordinary hackneyman was fixed at a penny a mile, 'or 1½ when he receiveth most', and 'journey's pace' is thus described in an Order by the Privy Council of Scotland (1613): 'that in the haill journey they sall go no bywayis, gallop, nor in any sort abuse the saidis joyrney horsis, utherwais than on the hieway quhair thair joyrney lyis from place to place to trott or pais out the way according to thair designe to thair joyrney's ende'.[1] It is easy to understand the disgust of the dashing hackneymen of Kent who had trained their horses to the 'Canterbury gallop'.

But on the whole, and certainly on the northern and western post-roads, the monopoly by bargain worked well enough to last for about fifty years, and achieved its purpose. It is true that it did not entirely obviate the necessity of raising wages. In 1557 upon 'complaint of the Posts northward that this busy time of the wars they are nothing able to live of 12*d*. by the day, which

[1] *Calendar of the Privy Council of Scotland* (1613).

in time of peace was their ordinary wages', the Privy Council raised their pay-rate to 1*s*. 8*d*., which remained thenceforward the standard rate in Elizabeth's reign. But the success of the scheme is to be seen in the fact that whereas at a shilling a day they had not been able to keep more than one horse, they could now, for 1*s*. 8*d*., be required to keep at least three, and after 1584 at least four. Thus though the Queen had to pay more, she was getting much better value for her money; and until the demand for rapid communications should have grown large enough to make the system entirely self-supporting, this was probably the best result that could have been achieved. The post-towns had some measure of relief, the posts managed to make a living, and the royal dispatches went forward at a reduced rate.

It has sometimes been assumed that since the Tudor posting system was created primarily for State purposes, the use made of it by the public was illicit. From what has been said it will be clear that this is a mistake. What was illicit was the use by private travellers of couriers' warrants entitling them to horses at a penny a mile. This had to be checked, since it would soon have made nonsense of the whole arrangement. But as long as the private traveller was prepared to pay the private rate of hire, his use of the Government post-stages (except in a national emergency) was not only permitted but encouraged, since the finance of the system depended on it. He could not, of course, *insist* upon being served with horses: only a holder of the Queen's warrant could do that. But in practice he could get them without unreasonable delay, and was thus able to enjoy for his money all the advantages that a post warrant would have secured.

The Tudor statesmen therefore deserve the credit of having turned a State necessity into something like a public benefit. Their motives may have been primarily to oil the wheels of their own administrative machine; but in effect they made it easier to summon a doctor, and easier for the doctor to come; easier for the debtor to abscond, and easier for the creditor to chase him; easier for young couples to elope, and easier for irate parents to enter in the nick of time crying 'Hold!' In short, they contributed to that general speeding up of the social and domestic scene which seems to distinguish the Elizabethan from earlier epochs.

XII

Duties of a Post

As a result of this bargain the posts found themselves charged with a two-fold duty, to the 'Packet' and to the 'Through Post', and their status was altered. Hitherto they had been regarded as Messengers of the Chamber on riding duty, and as such had, no doubt, been subject to the Messenger's rule that 'if he do send forth his man, boy or common carrier with any the letters of the Queen's Majesty, or of her Privy Council, he shall lose his service'.[1] But in view of their responsibility for the Through Post the men were now to be established 'at all times in such places in every town as that he that rideth post may have commodity of both lodging and meat and drink, if he wish to tarry'.[2] In other words, they were to be inn-keepers; and since an inn-keeper could not be expected to leave his inn to mind itself while he rode up and down with messages, it was recognized that the actual riding would have to be done by his servant or an approved deputy. Hence a change of title. Although 'post' was still the term used in all official documents before 1635, it became customary to give a post the courtesy title of 'postmaster', in order to distinguish him from his servant or deputy who did the riding. This courtesy title was challenged in 1582, when the Post of the Court, Robert Gascoigne, was charged with

[1] *Supplication of Lawrence Dutton and Raffe Walton* (1582). S.P. 12, CXXXV, 61.

[2] *Orders*, 1575 and 1583.

having arrogantly described himself as 'postmaster' in an official paper; but he replied that he was thus designated by members of the Council, and had a better right to the title 'than suche as be called post Mr of Rochester, Sithingbourn, Canterbury, or such like betwixt London and Barwick or elles where'. The term was evidently by this time in common use.[1]

No uniform is prescribed for a post-boy in any Elizabethan regulation. He appears as a wretchedly ill equipped ragamuffin who explains the fact that he has only got one spur by saying cheerfully that 'if the one side of his Jade goe forward, hee thinkes hee will not leave the other behind'.[2] A Messenger of the Chamber or royal courier was distinguished by the despatch box, stamped with the royal arms, that he carried slung from his shoulder; but the only articles of equipment prescribed for the humble post boy were his horn and his bag.

The horn became very important. In the earliest regulations he was required merely 'to blow it at the Town's end' as a warning to the next post, who, it was hoped, would thereupon saddle his horse and 'be ready to depart with the packet within one quarter of an hour after he heareth the boy or man blow his horn that bringeth it'. But the system seldom worked quite as smoothly as this, and in seeking the cause the Council always seems to have come to the conclusion that the boy had not blown his horn enough. By the end of the century he was required to blow it almost continuously. He was to blow it upon approaching any town; he was to blow it 'at all times' when he met people on the road, 'to warn them to give way unto the post', and even on a clear road, with nothing in sight, he was to blow it 'four times in every mile'. This last requirement seems unreasonable, but it is to be explained perhaps by a draft regulation of 1575 which provides that 'if this boy or man carrying the Queen's Majesty's packet be found sleeping upon the way, and complaint be made thereof by him that found him sleeping to the constable of that place where he dwelleth, or any other officer, and just trial made thereof: then pay to the poor man's box of the parish wherein he dwelleth, for every time *6s. 8d*'.[3]

[1] *The Answer of Robert Gascoigne . . . to Lawrence Dutton and others*. S.P. 12, CXXXV, 57.

[2] *Whimsies*, 1631 (A postmaster).

[3] *Orders devised for the Posts but not passed*, 1575.

Thus the horn was virtually the post-boy's taskmaster. He knew that any cessation of its sound might bring out idlers from the nearest hamlet to see if they could catch him napping. So he blew, and continued to blow, long and loud and virtuously.

The other piece of equipment prescribed for a post-boy was his bag. All posts were required to keep 'two leather bags lined with good cotton or baize, to carry their letters or packets in, to the end they may be kept clean and unbroken'. There was no trouble about this in Elizabeth's reign, but early in the seventeenth century dispatch-boxes began to be used for official correspondence, and these were sometimes too large to go into the bags usually provided. The post-boy of St. Alban's in 1652 explained the broken seals on a box of this kind by saying 'that his Master had no bag that would hold it', and that he therefore 'took his Master's girdle, and put the girdle under the pack-threads, and so broke the seals thereof, and also some part of the pack thread'.[1] Every post house between London and Towcester was badgered with questions about this unlucky packet, and we may be sure that before the end of the business the post of St. Albans was warmly advised by his colleagues to break his heart and buy a larger bag. Nothing was to be carried in the bag but 'letters or writings', and the boy was strictly forbidden 'to suffer any man to looke in his bag, to see what letters there are': an injunction which must sometimes have been difficult to observe on the desolate moors between Hexham and Haltwhistle when he met a gang of inquisitive outlaws.[2]

The writings to be carried in the bag were of two kinds: the 'Packet', which had to go forward 'within one quarter of an hour', and 'bye letters', which lacked official authority and must wait to be forwarded until an official 'Packet' ran. The Packet was sometimes a single letter, but more often a sealed bundle of letters, superscribed with the words 'for her Majesty's special affairs', and directed to or by some authorized person whose name had been notified to the posts. Unless it satisfied this description in all particulars it was not 'of sufficient warrant to constrain the posts to run' with it, and must be treated as a 'bye letter'.

[1] *Affidavit of John Davis, Post of Brickhill.* S.P. 14, CLXXXV, 20.

[2] Letters carried over this route often showed signs of having been opened. *S.P. Dom.* (Addenda 1547); Dasent IV, 142, and VI, 307.

The only persons authorized in 1575 to send packets, or to issue couriers' warrants, were the Earl Marshal, the President of the North, the three Wardens of the Borders and their deputies, the Master of the Posts, and any three Privy Councillors conjointly. The list was extended in 1584 to include the Lord Treasurer, the Governour of Berwick, the Principal Secretary, and the Warden of the Cinque Ports. But the marginal notes in Burghley's hand on the draft of these Orders show how jealously the privilege was guarded. The Earl Marshal was to enjoy it only *whilst he hath charge of the Queen of Scots*; the Lord Treasurer was to exercise it only *for the affairs of her Majesty's realm*; and the number of Councillors who could issue a warrant conjointly was raised emphatically from three to *'foore'*.[1]

Thus when Falstaff cries to Justice Shallow 'Let us take any man's horses. The laws of England are at my commandment', he is assuming an authority which it took four Privy Councillors to sustain, and is taking rank with an Earl Marshal or a Warden of the Cinque Ports.[2]

The persons named were authorized to send packets in post for her Majesty's special affairs, and, as a necessary corollary, to receive such packets from accredited correspondents, but nobody quite knew who these correspondents might be. They were usually persons who had been named by the Principal Secretary; but it was impossible for him to name every individual who might on occasion be legitimately employed upon correspondence of State, and difficulties often occurred. The mayors of sea-port towns, for instance, were often in doubt whether letters received from special agents abroad should go forward as 'packets' in their own right, or be treated as 'bye-letters'; even the correspondence of the Lord Deputy in Ireland, Montjoy, was sent as a 'packet' with some misgivings by the mayor of Chester in 1599, and in 1601 the post of Plymouth refused point blank to accept as 'packets' letters of the newly appointed Governour of the Work, Sir John Gilbert, alleging that he 'had no order for it'.[3]

[1] *Lansdowne MS.*, LXXVIII, 93.
[2] *Henry IV*, Pt. 2, V, iii, 138.
[3] *C.S.P. Dom* (1598–1601), pp. 281, 316, 396; (1601–3), p. 77; *H.M. Com. Cecil*, IX, 419; XI, 193.

In 1602 therefore an attempt was made to draft more precise instructions, while at the same time adding the Lord Admiral to the list; but the matter proved to be too intricate to be treated in detail, and the printed Orders of 1603 conclude with two general, and not very helpful, statements. Posts are to provide horses for the bearer of 'any Packet so directed, that it may appeare the partie despatched therewith rideth in our speciall affaires', and they are to accept as 'packets' letters addressed to the Secretaries, the Master of Posts, the Lord Admiral, the Warden of the Cinque Ports, the Treasurer and Secretary for Scotland and the Lord Deputy in Ireland 'in the proper business of their places, or to the body of our Counsell, from what persons or places whatsoever'.

Thus a good deal, after all, was left to the discretion of the men themselves. It cannot always have been easy to decide whether a letter addressed to one of these notables was addressed to him 'in the proper business of his place'. If it turned out to contain an offensive lampoon, for instance, the post who accepted it could get into very hot water 'for daring to send a packet without a councillor's hand to it'.[1] Such were the hazards of a post's calling.

If he was satisfied that the missive put into his hand was a genuine 'packet', his duty was first, to note and sign 'on the outside' the date and hour when it reached him, and secondly, to enter a full description of it in his ledger. This might appear a simple matter, but for some of the men it was probably the most ticklish part of the whole business. In the earliest surviving wage book of the posts, dated 1562, three of the men acknowledge receipt by making their marks, and several others sign their names with what is evidently excruciating difficulty.[2] It is therefore not surprising that the endorsements on Elizabethan packets are so often incomplete; and since, in the days before envelopes, they were made on the paper of the letter itself, it was not easy for the Postmaster to collect the information that would have enabled him to check the defaulters. The remedy was 'a labell annexed to the packet', first mentioned in 1582, and later described as 'a label of parchment or paper wherein the

[1] A libel of the Duke of Buckingham was thus accepted by the Post of Ware in 1617. *C.S.P. Dom* (1611–19), p. 480.

[2] *The Monethe Charges of the Posts. A.O.3*, 868.

packet may be wrapped'.[1] Randolph begs Walsingham in 1584 that 'if packets are not brought with such speed as they ought to be . . . you would reserve the scroll or covering, that thereby I may know the date, and seek out the fault'. Milton alludes to this scrap of paper in his *Lines on Hobson the Carrier*:

His letters are deliver'd all and gon,
Onely remains this superscription.

He is comparing his verses to the addressed scroll or wrapper, lying on the table of the deserted post room.

Having duly endorsed the packet and entered the particulars in his ledger, the post normally handed it over to his boy for conveyance to the next stage, but if it happened that a more mature and reliable traveller was going in the direction required the packet was sometimes entrusted to him. The practice was, of course, quite irregular. The post was forbidden 'to send a packet by any person whatsoever but by an expresse servant of his owne'. But against this it was always possible to plead the notorious irresponsibility of postboys. Even the Postmaster had had to admit that 'the negligence of servants and boys' had always been 'the greatest cause of the former disorders'.[2] Hence breaches of this rule were not always punished, and the post of Haltwhistle who entrusted a packet to 'three footmen' in 1596 was still serving in 1605.

For the invigoration of postboys it had become the custom as early as 1523, if not earlier, to write upon the outside of an urgent letter 'Haste, Post, haste for life'; meaning, probably, that he was to ride as if he were carrying 'a pardon to save one's life as he goeth to execution'. This had been found so effective that in 1559 Sir Ralph Sadler recommended it for all official letters. 'When we write', he says, 'we indorse our letters for life, though the matter require no such haste; and so must you do, or else the Posts will make no speed at all.'[3] The stimulus of these words, however (or of the more menacing version 'Hast, Post, hast, for thie lieff, lieff, lieff'), was only effective upon a post who could read. For the benefit of those who could

[1] *Orders set downe by commandement of the Quenes Matie*, 1582. S.P. 15, XXVIIA, 124. S.P. 12, CLXX, 7.

[2] Randolph's *Articles*, 1584. S.P. 12, CLXVII, 36.

[3] Sadler, II, 13.

not it became the practice, apparently not long before 1548, to add a rough sketch of the gallows with a dangling human figure. This embellishment was not sanctioned by any regulation, but it enabled an illiterate post-boy to distinguish at a glance between his urgent and less urgent letters.

Once mounted and on his way a post-boy's only remaining difficulty was to resist the temptation to deliver with his own hand some of the 'bye-letters' consigned to the post of the next stage, thus earning a tip or two, and recouping himself for the fact that the Packet went forward free of charge, and he would get no groat for his riding. But unless his master was prepared to connive, he had little hope of getting away with it. The posts, though not required to do so, had taken to entering the bye-letters in their ledgers as well as the Packets (no doubt as a check on such poaching) and the fault was bound to be discovered as soon as the books were compared. It was better for a post-boy to stick to virtue and relieve his feelings with an extra loud toot on his horn.

XIII

The Through Post and Private Posting

ON the whole a post's duties in relation to the Packet were straightforward and gave him little trouble, because he was dealing with people he knew. It was in connexion with the Through Post that most of his difficulties arose, because this brought him into contact with all sorts and conditions of men, some of them highly unpleasant.

A 'through post' was simply a man who rode 'through' with a missive. If it was a proclamation, writ, warrant, or any paper of such a kind that its delivery might have to be attested at law, he was a Pursuivant, Messenger of the Chamber, or other appropriate official. But the ordinary diplomatic correspondence was often carried by young courtiers who had begged the duty as a means of travelling cheap. Thus Robert Carvyle at Berwick begs the Scottish Ambassador in London 'that if it be needful that a through post should come up, it may be myself, for I would gladly be at Court to follow my suit'; and young Thomas Milles tells his uncle that he is going to make his fortune in Paris, because Randolph has promised 'to procure the Queen's packet and despatch me with the first; and when I am there let God and me alone'. A through post might be the son of an Ambassador going on furlough, or an army Captain rejoining his troop, or the future Master of Ceremonies, Lewkenor, going to see French fashions; and the large number of such amateurs to whom payments are recorded in the Chamber

Accounts suggests that the duty was regularly sought by young gentlemen who were sick of Court attendance and wanted to stretch their legs.[1] As messengers they were, no doubt, active and efficient, but as riders of other men's horses they must have been on the whole a pest. For it was hardly to be expected that a young man of this type would feel much concern either for his mount, or for the man who supplied it. Why should he? After weary months of being 'the Picture of Nobody' at Court he had suddenly been given precedence over every living thing on the Queen's highway. Even the Lord Chief Justice must get out of his way when his guide's horn sounded. Why should he consider anything or anybody but the figure he could cut and the speed he could make?

One of these Hotspurs, a certain Captain Winkfield, took up horses at Guildford in 1588, 'and although' says the mayor, 'the said Mr Winkfield was provided of a very good young gelding for his own riding, in such sort as none have or could be better furnished from the Town, yet riding in a very foul and dangerous way about three miles from the town, his gelding by some mishap fell with him, as the guide reporteth. Whereupon he presently, in some fury, thrust his dagger into the said gelding under the small ribs, whereof he died within one half hour, and beat the guide, threatening to kill him, and took from him the horse on which he rode, and sent him back again with threatening speeches that he would kill the constables at his return'.[2] The fact that this happened on 10 August, only a few hours after Drake's fire-ships had flushed the Armada from Calais, may explain the dispatch-rider's 'fury'. But that violent behaviour was characteristic of the through posts was a fact so well known that it could be used as an official threat. When the posts grew slack in performance of their duties they were told that 'the Queen's Majesty must be enforced to discharge them every one, and to seek some new means to be served from time to time with a through Post';[3] which meant, in effect, that instead of riding their horses themselves, they would be obliged to supply them at the Queen's price to riders like Captain Winkfield.

[1] *H.M. Com. Cecil,* III, 261; *Ashmole MS.,* 840, 75; *Chamber Accounts.*
[2] *Petition of the Mayor and Brethren of Guildford,* S.P. 12, CCXIV, 68.
[3] Dasent, VI, 385.

The professional messengers were probably less impetuous. But they were hard-bitten men who knew what was due to them, and had a short way with those who supplied them with inadequate horses. The post of Daventry complains in 1612 that he 'furnished Lewis Harris, pursuivant, with two able post-horses to Coventry, the way being verie foule and the wind troublesome, being in his face; and yet notwithstanding they carried him thither in two hours and a half, being XIlll miles. The said Lewis notwithstanding will not pay for my horses' hire, but abused me very greatly with slanderous speeches in Coventry, and at his return in Daventry, I demanding my money, did greatly abuse both me and my wife and whipped my servant over the face, and had not company aided, he had done more mischief unto my servant at Coventry. I humbly intreat your honour that some course may be taken with him, for I could have arrested his own horse which he brought from London to our Town of Daventry, but seeing that he did ride in his Mat's affairs I thought it not good in any case to stay him. And notwithstanding these abuses offered by him he threateneth to make an unjust complaint against me unto my Lord Treasurer'.[1] The incident is typical, and illustrates the point upon which these disputes usually turned.

There was no question, of course, but that horses supplied under the Queen's warrant were to be paid for. It was emphasized in all the regulations, and asserted in the warrant itself, which either specified the rate of hire or stated that the horses were to be supplied 'at reasonable and accustomed prices'. This clause might be omitted in the warrant issued to an Ambassador or other distinguished person whose expenses were to be 'defrayed' by the Queen. In the order for horses to be supplied to the Duke of Biron in 1601 the words were 'by Mr. Secretary Cecil's direction left out'. But this merely meant that the Duke was not to be dunned for the hire, not that the horses were to be supplied *gratis*, for five days later the principal courier for France was paid £24. 12*s*. for the hire of the hackneys supplied.[2] There were no real exceptions to the rule, and in so far as pursuivant Harris was simply refusing to pay, he was clearly in the wrong and had not a leg to stand on.

[1] *William Clerke to the Secretary*, 10 April 1612, S.P. 14, LXVIII, 96.
[2] Dasent, XXXII, 205, 209.

On the other hand a post-warrant always stipulated for 'hable and sufficient horses', and this phrase opened a door to controversy. What was a 'sufficient' horse? The ideal horse contemplated by the regulations was apparently one which could be ridden at the rate of seven miles an hour in summer and five in winter, for anything above this pace was defined as 'unreasonable riding'. But it was not clear how far a horse might fall short of this standard without ceasing to be in the official sense 'sufficient'. The only positively insufficient horse of which the regulations took cognizance was the one which, though reasonably ridden, died under its rider before reaching the next stage.

In such a case it was gravely laid down that the rider should be liable for hire only up to the point of the animal's decease.[1] But between this calamitous beast and the flier at seven miles an hour the regulations left everything to conjecture, and enabled town authorities to argue that any old hunk of hounds' meat that could shamble over the stage without actually dropping in its tracks was a 'sufficient' horse within the meaning of the regulations. The professional courier's ideas on the subject were naturally very different, and what made him tenacious of his opinion was his knowledge that the authorities could easily find him something fit to ride if they thought him worth the attention. Every copy of Elizabethan regulations contained the statement that the post was empowered to 'take up' horses in case of need (which was allowed to mean if his own were inadequate), and that in this he was to be assisted by the town authorities. The courier provided with a poor hack knew that if they had regarded him as 'a man of countenance' they would have taken up some gentleman's gelding for his use. It was therefore natural that he should take it as a reflection on his status, object to it as 'insufficient', refuse to pay for it, threaten the stablemen, and in short cut up rough. The whole problem of the 'sufficient' horse thus became so delicate, and so heavily fraught with occasion of offence, especially when the courier was some conceited young courtier who had begged the duty, that it wasted hours of riding time.

'Lord Ker, the earl of Roxburgh's son, riding post the other day into the North, having letters from the Queen, came to Ware, and the postmaster went out to take up three horses for

[1] *Orders*, 1575, embodying a rule laid down by the Patent of 1396.

his use: but out of malice would have taken a great carthorse which carried corn to the market, only the owner, a poor countryman, would not part with it, saying the horse was not to ride post. The postmaster and he being in strife together in the market, three Deputy Lieutenants, Justices of the Peace, namely Sir Richard Lucy, Sir John Butler and Sir John Watts, convening there about county business, saw this contention out of a window of the inn, and they relieved the countryman, bidding the postmaster seek out other horses more fit for the service; whereupon the postmaster, in a great chafe, goes back to Lord Ker and tells him the Deputy Lieutenants had taken one of those horses he had taken up by his warrant. Lord Ker frets at this, and learns where the Deputy Lieutenants' horses stand, and commands three of these horses to be saddled to ride post with.

'The Deputy Lieutenants have notice of this, and will not let their horses be saddled; whereupon a great contention ensued between the Lord and these Deputy Lieutenants. So hot grew Lord Ker, who had a case of pistols by his side, that he and his two men challenged the three Justices into the field to end the difference.

'Sir John Butler and Sir John Watts had good stomachs to go out with them; but Sir Richard Lucy, a more temperate man, would rather use his authority than his courage that way, as being much the more justifiable course; and so sent out to provide post horses for them, which were brought to the gate. Sir Richard then tells Lord Ker there are the post horses for him, and, if he will not take them, himself will make his Lordship fast and take from him the Queen's letters, send them to his Majesty, and do his errand, which would be little to his Lordship's advantage.

'Whereupon he Lord Ker cools a little and, grumbling at being thus thwarted, takes the horses provided for him, and away he posts'.[1]

Another difficulty arose from irregular warrants, issued by personages who thought themselves important enough to risk it, and wished to get cheap travelling facilities for their relatives. The authority to issue such warrants was, as has been said, strictly confined to certain officers of State and members of the

[1] Quoted by Hyde, p. 170.

Privy Council. But there was nothing to prevent some court official from writing to the authorities of a neighbouring town, and asking, as a favour, that horses might be supplied to the bearer of his very important missive; and such a document was not easy to deal with. It is true that it was not likely to get horses at the cheap rate from a Government post who knew his business; but presented at some place where there was no post stage, and nobody had a list of the authorized persons, it might easily acquire the force of a regular warrant. Thus in 1598 an unauthorized warrant of this kind, signed by the Lords Thomas Howard and Montjoy, was presented by a certain John Howard —not at Crewkerne, the regular post stage for this section of the western road—but at Chard, eight miles west of it. The Bailiff of Chard, no doubt intimidated by the great names on the paper, took up the necessary horses, but probably stipulated (as was usual) that they should be ridden only to the next post stage and no further. John Howard, however, 'beinge on his way, did beate the guide and went away with the horses'.[1] Why? Because it would have been useless to present a bogus warrant at a regular post stage. His game was to skip the regular stages, and take his horses at intermediate places where bluff might get them at the cheap rate. With any luck he would save nine shillings on his ride to London, and by dodging the ordinary posting stables might hope to get better horses to ride.

Attempts to travel without paying the proper fare are of course common at any time, but in the sixteenth and seventeenth centuries they were perhaps particularly liable to occur because of the high cost of posting.

[1] Dasent., XXVIII, 561, 563.

XIV

Cost and Speed of Posting

THE cost of posting was indeed formidable. During Elizabeth's reign the rate rose from 1*d.* to 2½*d.* a mile for commissioned riders, and from 2*d.* to 3*d.* for private travellers. This was payable on at least two horses, and the guide (who would carry luggage up to 40 lb. in weight) was entitled to a groat at each stage, apart from tips. Tips however were advisable, otherwise you might find your horse 'loosely saddled, or budget carelessly trussed'.

In 1584, when the rates stood at 1½*d.* for riders with commission and 2*d.* for those without, the posting charges from London were as follows: to Berwick 72*s.* 4*d.* with commission and 93*s.* 10*d.* without; to Chester 36*s.* 8*d.* and 47*s.* 8*d.*; to Bristol 29*s.* 3*d.* and 37*s.*; to Plymouth 47*s.* 3*d.* and 61*s.* 8*d.*, and to Dover (at a flat rate of 2*s.* 6*d.* a stage) 26*s.* 8*d.* Translated into modern money these charges would be a good deal higher than the present fares for travel by air. More than half of the expense arose from the compulsory employment of the guide; but this was inevitable as long as so many of the horses used were requisitioned from private stables. To have one's horse taken 'to run post' was always felt as a bitter grievance, and the least that the Government could do was to guarantee that it should not be ridden beyond the next stage, and should promptly be returned. Hence the necessity of the guide, and the emphasis laid by all the Elizabethan regulations on the obligation to employ him. It was not until the posts began to keep larger stables that posting without guides became possible. In a proposal of 1616 for an extension of the posting system in Scotland it is provided that

> 'To spair unnecessar charges to his Majesties lieges, and that no necessitie of boyes or other attendantes go with the jorney horsis, giff possibly it can be . . . the Maister of Poistes sall have speciale cair that sic correspondence be amange the jorney maisteres that lyis maist adjacent togidder, that ilkane of thame on reasonable conditiones sall cair for utheris horses resorting to thame, intertaine thame, and use thame kyndlie, and keip reciprocation togidder, ayther in back-reconducing of thame as the commoditie sall offer, or detening thame sum schort space'.[1]

In England the first reference to such an obviously sensible arrangement occurs in the *Orders* of 1635, which instruct the traveller that 'if he shall have occasion but for one horse, then to leave him at the place where he shall take fresh horses, paying for him 2½*d*. for every mile; if two horses, then to take a guide and pay 5*d*. a mile.'[2]

Until this concession was made the only way of avoiding the expense of a mounted guide was to time one's journey so as to ride with the postboy who carried the Packet. This was the common practice of travellers to the Continent, who used the Flanders Post as guide, and it was advertised as a regular facility by the enterprising posts of the Plymouth road in 1629. They undertook to provide post-horses for all that will ride with the Letters for single post-pay from stage to stage, *viz*. for 2½*d*. the mile, without further charge except 4*d*. to the guide for the return of his (the traveller's) horse.[3] But the amount that could be saved in this way obviously depended on the endurance, not to say the heroism, of the traveller. To ride 'with the letters' all the way from London to Plymouth would have meant more than fifty-two hours in the saddle. In practice the traveller probably rode with the post boy on the first day of his journey, and continued thereafter at the ordinary posting rate with a paid guide. In this way he might reduce his posting fare to Plymouth, which stood at 92*s*. 8*d*. at the date of this

[1] *Register of the Privy Council of Scotland*, X, 836.
[2] *A Proclamation for the Settling of a Letter Office*, July 1635.
[3] *H.M. Com. City of Exeter*, p. 66.

concession, to something like £4. But even at £4, representing, as it probably does, about £25 of our money, it was an expensive way of travelling to Plymouth.

The speed of posting varied with the social eminence of the traveller, for this was allowed to affect the question whether horses should be requisitioned for him from a private stable or not. The rule was that 'hable and sufficient' horses should be provided; but what was deemed 'sufficient' for a social nobody might be very far from 'sufficient' for a personage like Sir Thomas Gorges, who, on being provided in Exeter with horses 'such as carry wood up and down the town', reported the Mayor to the Council for contempt of the Queen's warrant.[1] A post was often obliged for social reasons to requisition better horses than his own, and in doing so had the full support of the Postmaster.

'I must crave all lawful favour', writes Randolph to Davison in 1586, 'in behalf of the Post and Constable of Ware (who had taken up a horse belonging to the Victualler General), and if the cause befor taking up of Mr. Quarles's horse to serve a throughpost at a time of necessity, surely I see not how they are to be blamed, seeing I know not him or any other at such times exempted from her Majesty's service'.[2]

There were, of course, limits to be observed by a prudent man. A constable who had the nerve to take up the Earl of Salisbury's horse in 1612 was sent to the Marshalsea to reflect upon the importance of tact in public life.[3] But tact might cut both ways; and the following postscript added by Randolph to a post-warrant for the Somerset herald in 1582 makes it clear that a post was not allowed to be timid in this matter:–

> I do specially recommend him unto you all, that for his own saddle you find him horses the best that you can, and if your own horses be not good, that then you provide him with such as shall sufficiently serve his turn. This I require at your hands because as a special friend of mine I would have him speed the better for my sake.[4]

The speed made by distinguished or favoured persons is therefore apt to be misleading. Prince Henry could post the sixty-three miles from Richmond to Huntingdon in nine hours, and

[1] *C.S.P.Dom* (1596–7), p. 73.
[2] Randolph to Davison, 13 Nov. 1586. S.P. 12, CXCV, 14.
[3] *The humble petition of Richard Nicholls*. S.P. 14, LXIX, 37.
[4] *Ashmole MS.*, 1113. *fol.* 108.

the Master of Ceremonies once covered the forty-nine miles between Dover and Gravesend in seven.[1] But these are mentioned as exceptional performances, and it is probable that better horses than usual were supplied. The same may be said of the remarkable journey made in 1601 by Roger Boyle, son of the Earl of Cork. He left Shannon Castle, near Cork, with news of the victory at Kinsale at 2 a.m. on Monday morning, and supped with Sir Robert Cecil on Tuesday (presumably before midnight), having travelled more than 320 miles in something under forty-six hours.[2] An even higher average speed was made by Richard Hawkins in 1586. He landed at St. Michael's Mount with news of the sacking of Carthagena, and rode the 110 miles to Exeter in fourteen hours, thus maintaining an average of nearly eight miles an hour over some of the worst going in England.[3] But there were no post-stages west of Exeter at this date, and every horse he rode must have been provided by a private stable. As for the record-breaking John Lepton who in 1605 is said to have posted five times between London and York in the course of a single week, and to have maintained, on at least one of his journeys, the astonishing average of twelve miles an hour, I take it for granted that he used quite exceptional horses, probably lent by sporting gentlemen who were betting on the result.[4]

Riding their own horses in the ordinary routine of their duties the posts were expected to maintain a speed of seven miles an hour in summer and five in winter; but if we may judge by the Elizabethan letters upon which the endorsements are clear and reasonably complete, they seldom if ever did as well as this. Of eighteen such letters carried over the Exeter road between 1595 and 1604 the fastest travelled the 135 miles from Exeter to Hartford Bridge at 6½ miles an hour, and the average for the group is 4.7. Twenty letters from Dover to Dartford during the same period travelled at an average of 4.6, four from Bristol to Newbury at 4.3, and four from Nantwich to St. Albans at an average of 5.1. Of the forty-six letters noted only six (two from Exeter and four from Dover) travelled

[1] Nichols. *Progresses of King James*, II, 458; *Finetti Philoxenis*, 1656, p. 75.
[2] Eustace Budgell. *Memoirs of . . . the Earl of Orrery*, 1732, p. 14.
[3] Letter of John Fitz to Walsingham. *H.M. Com. Rutland*, I, 200.
[4] Stow. *Abridgement of the English Chronicle*, p. 455.

faster than 6 miles an hour, and the general average is 4.6.[1]

Captain Plume, Farquhar's *Recruiting Officer*, described four miles an hour as 'pretty smart riding'; but he was probably thinking of a journey made on a cavalry mount, with a spare horse led by an orderly. With frequent change of horses a speed of 4.6 miles an hour seems rather poor going. It is clearly not 'how they brought the good news from Ghent to Aix'. But it is to be remembered that it is an average, based on computed, not measured, miles, maintained over long distances, by night as well as by day, through a country entirely unlit after dark, and along roads which, when not pestered with sloughs or loose stones, often dwindled over heaths and open farm land into a vague and uncharted right of way. A post boy benighted in such country might spend miserable hours dismounting to feel for cart ruts, turning his coat inside out to defeat Robin Goodfellow, listening for the murmur of a remembered brook or the clinking chains of a never to be forgotten gibbet; and it would not be until the blessed sun rose upon him that he would become once more his habitual self: 'a ragged villain, all bemired, upon a poor lean jade, riding and blowing for life'.[2]

[1] Letters selected from *H.M. Com. Cecil*, and *C.S.P. Dom.*

[2] 'The Ordinary post boy of London' as he appeared in an entertainment given at the Tiltyard in 1595. Devereux. *Lives of the Earls of Essex*, I, 317.

XV

Breakdown of the Bargain

THE monopoly by bargain was an ingenious arrangement which seems to have worked well as long as the volume of dispatches remained moderate and reasonably constant. As long as a post could forecast the amount of the penny a mile work that he would have to do, he could calculate the number of horses he must keep in order to retain his hold on the private passenger traffic. But it was an inherent defect of the scheme that any large and sudden increase in the volume of official correspondence might produce a situation in which the post would be compelled to keep all his horses at work at a penny a mile, while all the profitable jobbing went to other hackneymen in the town.

This happened in 1566 and again in 1573, chiefly owing to abuse of the power to grant commissions. Until 1573 a post warrant might, by a Statute of Edward VI, be granted by any two Privy Counsellors conjointly, and it appears that, like the 'franking' of letters at a later period, the privilege had been freely used to oblige friends and relatives. It was found necessary to increase the number of persons who could issue a warrant conjointly, and in 1578 to rule 'that from henceforth no Letters of Commissions to ride in post should be written to be subscribed by any of their Lordships unless the same were first moved at the Council Table, or directed by the Secretary for causes properly appertaining to H.M. service'.[1]

[1] Dasent, VII, 326.

But by 1584 it had become apparent that the volume of official correspondence by post and courier was now too large for the posts to handle on the old basis. If they had had security of tenure they might perhaps have been able to keep larger stables. But their wage bill was over £3,400 a year, and the Queen could never bring herself to keep them in pay a moment longer than necessary. On the great north road, it is true, troubles on the Border and her fears of what might proceed from Scotland induced her to keep them in pay throughout her reign; but on all the four western roads, to Chester, Bristol, Plymouth and Portsmouth, the posts were engaged or dismissed as the danger of Spanish invasion or Irish rebellion loomed or waned. An Elizabethan post was therefore never, except perhaps on the Dover road, in a position to venture much capital in his business. He could never be sure that at the month's end he might not find himself deprived, by a stroke of the pen, of both wages and monopoly, and compelled to sell off his spare horses at a moment when other men on the road were doing the same thing, and prices were falling.

His finances were further bedevilled by a system of exactions. First, he had to buy his place from the Master of the Posts; usually by remitting his first year's pay. Out of his pay, when he got it, he was mulcted 2*s.* in the pound to provide a fee for the Paymaster, 40*s.* for a mysterious Treasury charge called 'Orders', and 2*s.* 6*d.* on every acquittance, making a total charge of about £5. 10*s.* on his salary of £30. 6*s.* 8*d.* And as though this was not enough, he was expected from time to time to present the Master of the Posts with a 'Benevolence': ostensibly a freewill gift, but actually, perhaps, a *douceur* to prevent the Master from inquiring too closely into his perquisites. 'I am credibly informed' writes the mischief making Lord Hunsdon to Burghley in 1587, 'that whenever Mr. Randall doth put in a Post, he keeps his first year's wages to himself, so as the poor man serves a whole year for nothing. And besides he hath a yearly pension of every one of them, of some 40*s.*, £3, £5, and of some more; and I know that when he went into Muscovia' (as Ambassador in 1568) 'he had of every Post £20, so as I marvel how they are able to have and keep their horses'.[1]

The finances of the posts had thus always been somewhat

[1] *Calendar of Border Papers*, I, 298.

precarious, and by 1584 it had become clear that if they were to keep going they would have to be subsidized in some way.

It had long been the custom in some towns, lying on busy high roads, to keep a few horses ready for an emergency by levying a town rate. These arrangements, which have been noted at Leicester, Nottingham, Norwich, St. Alban's and Newcastle,[1] seem to have been promoted by the inn keepers to ensure the safety of their guests' horses. A common innkeeper was responsible for the property of the traveller lodging in his inn, and as the law then stood, could not limit his liability by any declaration of 'owner's risk'. If therefor a traveller's horse was taken from an inn stable to run post, and in consequence was injured or destroyed, an action lay against the innkeeper. It is true that if the horse had been taken up for the Queen's service the Privy Council might be prepared to quash proceedings by simply commanding the luckless owner of the horse to drop his suit.[2] But such incidents were bad for the reputation of an inn, and it seems to have been generally admitted that inn keepers were in a difficult position. When Officials of the Mint refused horses to the Post of London in 1591, the Council accepted it as a real grievance that he was thereby enforced 'to take up horses in inns and such like places, to his own great danger and hindrance'.[3] And the word 'danger' was not merely rhetorical. The chief London inn keepers were paying an 'annual Benevolence' to the Post of Bishopsgate (certainly by 1619 and probably earlier) 'to spare their guests' horses from his Majesty's service',[4] and their ostlers were capable of giving him a very warm reception if, after accepting this baksheesh, he dared to enter their stables. 'First, your Honour's commission was throwed down on the ground', complains the Post of Bishopsgate who tried to take up horses at the *Green Dragon* in 1625; next, 'he had his legs taken from him, was beaten and baffled about the head and face (as is apparent), lost his hat and purse with xxxs and an ob in it, and had his clothes all rent and torn'. When he went on to try for better

[1] *H.M. Com. St Alban's*, p. 566; *Records of the Borough of Nottingham*, Stevenson 1882, III, 391; *Records of the Borough of Leicester* (Bateson, 1923), III, 66, 77, 125; *Records of the City of Norwich* (Hudson and Tingey, 1910), II, 135.

[2] Dasent, XI, 47; XIX, 66; XXVIII, 563.

[3] Dasent, XXI, 119.

[4] *Certificate of John King*. S.P. 14, CX, 139.

luck at the *White Hart* he found them waiting for him 'as though they had conspired it before', and he was 'assaulted, beaten and misused in both places'.[1]

This was the London inn keepers' way of guaranteeing the safety of their stables, and it is probable that the provincial arrangements were designed as a more pacific method of attaining the same result. At Norwich the inn keepers paid half the cost of the scheme between them; and the contract for keeping eight geldings ready at St. Alban's expressly stipulates 'that all strangers, and others not inhabitants within the same borough shall be discharged thereof, and their geldings, mares and horses not to be taken for the service at any time'.

Rates in aid of the post were thus already customary in some towns, and the Privy Council now began to promote such arrangements by ordering contributions, either in horses or money, to be made, at first by the hundreds adjacent to the post roads, and ultimately by the whole county. The first county rate in aid of the post was ordered in Warwickshire in 1601.[2]

But this method was very unsatisfactory to the public. It was one thing to pay money for keeping horses in your own town as an insurance against disturbance: it was quite another to pay some fellow at the other side of the county for keeping horses which would insure you against nothing. The inhabitants of Atherstone, for instance, who had duly paid the rate for keeping horses at Coleshill, the regular post stage, twenty miles away, would not thereby escape having to provide horses at a penny a mile if some courier, riding for Chester in wet weather, decided to keep the line of Watling Street, and presented his 'placart' at Atherstone. They would really be paying the same mulct twice over.

The reluctance to contribute was therefore so strong that the Government seems to have been driven to adopt the cynical expedient of making the posts their own collectors. Hitherto a post had had no power to requisition until the traveller's warrant was put into his hand; but it now became the practice to furnish him with a 'warrant dormant', empowering him to take up horses (or money in lieu of horses) at will within a specified area. In effect, he could now walk into a harvest field and exact a

[1] *Complaint of Thomas Moreton*. E. 15, XLIII, 135.
[2] Dasent, XIX, 166; XXV, 538; XXX, 568; XXXII, 194, 303, 391.

payment from the farmer for not taking his horses out of the shafts.[1] Having thus provided the posts with a weapon of blackmail, and reduced them to the condition of those sharking 'purveyors' who had been such a nuisance in the fifteenth century, the Government seems to have felt that it had done enough for them, and allowed their pay to fall steadily into arrears. In 1628 their wages were seven years overdue, and the amount owing to them was £22,000: by 1630 it had risen to £25,000, and by 1637 is said to have stood at £60,000.[2] It seems clear that if the men had been wholly dependent on their pay the posting system would have completely broken down during this period. It survived partly because the 'monopoly by bargain' had in many cases enabled the post to establish a successful livery stable business, and partly because the perquisites that he could pick up in the exercise of his duty had now grown so large that they were worth more to him than his pay.

[1] For instances of the misuse of these warrants see Hyde *The Early History of the Post*, pp. 55, 146, 153.

[2] *C.S.P. Dom* (1629–31), p. 379.

XVI

Bye Letters

A POST was often required to deliver a packet at some place distant from his regular stage. Sir Ralph Saddler's commission in 1569, for instance, was addressed 'To our trustie and wel-beloved Sir Rauff Sadleyr, Knight, Hert. Post of Ware, se this lettre delivered' (i.e. at Standon, three miles off the road), and a letter of 1594, addressed to Lord Cobham, bears on the back a request to the post of Rochester: 'Mr. Bowls, I pray you cause this letter to be sent to his Lordship' (presumably at Cobham, five miles away), 'it concerneth his Lordship's special affairs'.[1]

When deliveries of this kind became a frequent and exacting part of a post's duties, he was able to secure a special allowance from the Postmaster. The post of Wetherby, for instance, drew an additional 7*d.* or 1*s.* a day (according to the pressure of business) for delivering packets to the President of the Council in York; and similar allowances were made to the posts of Grantham and Stilton during the imprisonment of the Queen of Scots at Chartley and Tutbury.[2] But as a rule a post drew no extra pay for delivery of a packet, which was regarded as part of his routine duty, and all that he could hope for was a gratuity from the person to whom it was directed. This however was almost certain to be forthcoming. Innumerable entries in Tudor and Stuart account books show that whenever a private servant

[1] Sadler. II, p. 13; *H.M. Com. Cecil*, IV, p. 475.
[2] P.O. Accounts.

arrived at a gentleman's door with a present, letter or verbal message, it was regarded as proper to give him a 'reward', assessed not so much on the importance of his errand as upon the social eminence of the person who had sent him. This etiquette was bound to operate very favourably for the posts, because they could claim to represent the most eminent person in the land, but also for the quite different, but equally cogent, reason that they made so much noise: a point of some importance. It might be possible to dispose of the quiet blue-coated fellow who brought a present of game from a relative with, say, a shilling and a drink in the buttery; but when a Government post clattered into the yard, waking the echoes with his horn, there was no evading the obligation to come down handsome.

This was so well understood that if a post omitted for some reason to blow his horn at a gentleman's door, it could be taken as a slur on his character or solvency. A certain Mr. Phillips, Clerk of the Tents and Hales, was sadly nettled by an incident of this kind in 1554. 'Pleaseth yt your worshipe to be advertysyd', he writes to the Master, Sir Thomas Cawarden, 'that yester nyght there came a post frm the Corte with two letters; the one the post brought with a horne about hys nek, blowing as he came throwgh old Fyshe Streete, to Mr. Hale; the other was browght unto us to the Blake Fryers with sylence'.

Now Mr. Hale was only Groom of the Tents at £5 a year, while he, as Clerk, had a fee of £13. 6*s*. 8*d*. and everything handsome about him. It was very vexing. 'I wolde not have stykyd to have gevyn the post a crown', he continues, 'to have had one blaste blowen with his horne at my dore for honors sake'.[1] A crown is evidently mentioned here as a very lavish and handsome reward, and one may infer that a post usually got less on these occasions. But even if it was no more than half a crown or a florin, it might in the course of a year make a useful supplement to a wage of £30. 6*s*. 8*d*., and it was only natural that he should consider the possibility of augmenting it by undertaking to deliver private letters in the same dashing style.

Private letters, or 'Bye letters' as they were then called, are officially recognized for the first time in the *Articles* drawn up by Randolph in 1584, which prescribe:

[1] *The Loseley Manuscripts*, ed. Kempe, 1836, p. 100.

'That no Posts servant or boy, riding with the Packet shall deliver any bye letters or private packets before he have first discharged himself of the Packet for her Majesty's affairs, he delivering the same unto the hands of the next standing Post. Unto whom also he shall commit and deliver all the bye letters and private packets as well as the other, upon pain of the forfeiture of ten shillings to the Post offended, and the displeasure of the Master of the Posts.

That no post's servant or boy, riding with the Packet and having bye letters or private packets or other kind of carriage committed unto them, shall adventure to open or break up or any other ways directly or indirectly shall fraudulently embezzle or convey the same wilfully, but shall safely deliver the same unto the hands of the next Post, as is aforesaid. And whatsoever he be that shall be found to be faulty herein, he shall lose his Master's service, and the Master shall underlie such punishment as the Master of the Posts shall find him worthy of'.

It is clear from this that by 1584 the carriage of private letters had become such a large part of the posts' activities that it had begun to interfere with the Packet; that the delivery of private letters in and near a post town was regarded as an important perquisite of the post there placed; and that the competition for these lucrative deliveries had grown so keen that the men had to be restrained from 'sorting' each others' packets and poaching on each others' preserves. What charge may have been made for accepting a private packet for conveyance by post is not stated, but it does not appear that the Master of the Posts had any financial interest in the business. It was expressly stated before a committee of the Privy Council in 1633 that 'neither the Lord Stanhope, nor any other that ever enjoyed the Postmaster's place of England, had any benefit of carrying and recarrying of the subject's letters'.[1] His intervention in 1584 seems to have been simply for the purpose of securing priority for the Queen's Packet, and keeping the peace between his men.

It is doubtful, however, whether his success was more than temporary. During the next twenty years the private packet business increased so much and got so seriously out of hand that in 1603 the posts were found to be regularly using the horses which should have been kept ready for the Queen's

[1] *A Proposition for settling of Staffets*, 1635, printed in the Report of the Secret Committee on the Post Office, 1844.

Packet in the express delivery of private letters, and had so far lost their sense of the distinction between official and private correspondence that they were actually entering the latter in their monthly returns to the Master of the Posts. It was found necessary in that year to order that no letters 'be sent or carried expressly in post but the Queen's Packets only', that a post was not to be employed 'out of the ordinary way of this stage above two miles', and that he was to enter in his ledger 'only such for our Packets as come warranted as aforesaid' (i.e. by certain officials) 'and all others to pass as Bye letters'. The last clause makes it clear that the Government had no objection to the carriage of private letters in post, provided that the horses kept for the Packet were not turned out expressly to carry them. In other words bye letters or private packets must be held over until an official Packet ran, and might then be forwarded in the same bag.

During the reign of King James, as the posts' pay began to fall heavily into arrears, their effective income came to depend more and more upon what they could make by this private packet business; and it happened that the posts on the London Plymouth road found themselves in a position greatly to extend it.

It was the regular custom for ships homeward bound from ports in Spain and the Levant to touch at Plymouth in order to land supercargoes and agents, who thereupon posted up to London with their bills of lading and letters of advice. Advance news of this kind was eagerly awaited by the merchants, and the play called *Englishmen for my Money*[1] gives a lively sketch of the excitement on the Exchange when one of these messengers arrived.

Enter a Post

WALGRAVE. Hoyda! Hoyda! What's the matter now?
HARVIE. Sure, yonder fellow will be torn in pieces.
What's he, sweet youths, that they so flock about
What! Old Pisaro tainted with this madness!
HEIGHAM. Upon my life! 'tis somebody brings news;
The Court breaks up, and we shall know their counsel
Look! Look! How busily they fall to reading!

One of the merchants turns to the Post with an inquiry:

[1] Printed 1616, but entered in the Stationers' Register, 1601.

I prithee when thinkst thou the Ships will come about from Plymouth?

POST. Next week, sir.

HEIGHAM. Came you, sir, from Spain lately?

POST. Ay sir. Why ask you that?

HEIGHAM. Marry, sir, thou seems to have been in the hot countries, thy face looks so like a piece of rusty Bacon.

The skinflint Pisaro has bad news, and at first turns a deaf ear to the Post's request for a gratuity; but hearing from an Italian merchant, who has later advices, that his ships are safe after all, he impulsively gives the Post a French crown.

POST. Marry, God bless your worship; I came in happy time!
What, a French crown! Sure, he knows not what he does
Well, I'll begone, lest he remember himself, and take it from me again.

At the time when this was written (1601) posting facilities between Plymouth and London were evidently important to merchants trading in the Levant, and with the growth of that trade in the early years of the seventeenth century they must have become daily more necessary. How they were maintained from 1611 to 1620, when no Government stages existed on that road, can only be conjectured. But it is probable that the merchants, who were allowed to use posts of their own, had stretched the privilege by contracting for relays of horses at the chief towns on the road, and it seems to have been the persistence or increase of such arrangements after 1620, when the regular Government stages were reestablished, that provoked the posts to take action. In 1626 a certain Samuel Jude, 'being a tradesman of London and of good estate, and keeping many horses here and there upon the road, what with the help of others, and two of his servants travelling weekly between London and Plymouth', began 'under pretence of carrying private letters' (i.e. for the merchants) to take upon him 'the speedy dispatch of men's private packets with other post business'.[1]

It was a manifest invasion of the posts' monopoly, for none but they might legally hire out horses to 'run the gallop' from stage to stage; and it was a dangerous piece of poaching, for

[1] *Petition of his Ma? Posts of the Western Stages*, 19 Feb. 1629. S.P. 16, CLXI, 27. (Misdated 1630. See *H.M. Com. City of Exeter*, p. 66.)

Jude was evidently trying to annex the private packet business which had long been the posts' allowed perquisite.

The challenge was so serious that it suggested to Thomas Hutchins of Crewkerne, and his fellow posts on that road, the idea of forming a syndicate and offering the merchants an express service of their own between London and Plymouth. For this it was clear that official sanction would be necessary. The posts were still bound by the regulation of 1603, which forbade them to turn out their horses 'expressly' to run with bye letters; and unless this rule could be relaxed, their scheme would be at the mercy of any jealous informer. But if they could get permission to carry even one 'express' private packet in and out every week, they would be in a position to secure the merchants' contract, and with this as a nucleus might hope greatly to extend the miscellaneous letter carrying which had become an essential part of their livelihood.

Thomas Hutchins deserves to be remembered in the history of the Post Office. He was a busy, truculent and evidently very capable man who had gained such an ascendancy over the Posts that they had submitted, under his leadership, to something like Trade Union organization, and paid regular contributions to a central fund. With the money thus supplied Hutchins had agitated vigorously on their behalf for payment of their arrears of pay, and upon the appointment of Charles, Lord Stanhope, to succeed his father, Lord John, as Master of the Posts in 1621, had opened a regular campaign of complaint against the exactions of the Postmaster and his subordinates the Paymasters. It was no longer merely a matter of the old grievances about 'poundage', 'Orders' and 'Acquittance fees'. The new Postmaster had (very incautiously) demanded that the Posts, who had duly bought their places from Lord John, should now buy them over again from him. These mulcts were politely called 'Fines on Admittance', and they had given Thomas Hutchings his chance. By dint of loud clamour and persistent lobbying he had managed to get the Postmaster's exactions reviewed by a committee of the Privy Council, and had won a resounding victory. The 'poundage' of 2*s*. had been reduced to 6*d*.; the charge of 40*s*. for 'Orders' had been abolished; the charge of 2*s*. 6*d*. on every acquittance had been reduced to 1*s*. ('if any thing at all'); and as for fines on admittance upon the change of

Postmaster, the committee had found 'no cause why they should be paid, being a verie great burthen'.[1] True, the Council had followed this up by ordering that the posts should no longer 'employ as their solicitor Thomas Hutchins, who has so importuned the Council by his clamours that he is ordered to be committed if he appear before them again'. But this had done nothing to impair his prestige with the posts. And now Thomas Hutchins was approaching his masterpiece. He was asking leave to demonstrate that the mechanism of the royal Packet, which had always been regarded by everyone concerned as a deplorable but inevitable expense of Government, could, if properly worked, become a source of revenue. In other words, he was proposing to found the modern postal system. None of the responsible officials seem to have thought much of the scheme. Lord Stanhope and the Paymaster, Mr. Dolliver, were inclined to oppose it as bad for postal discipline. But it seems to have presented itself to the Council as an unimportant concession which, if granted, might do something to stop the incessant clamour of these noisy western posts for their arrears of pay. The application was therefore successful, and on 21 November 1629 Hutchins and his men secured an Order in Council authorizing them to 'undertake the speedy dispatch of all private letters weekly from London to Plymouth and from Plymouth to London', the delivery of letters 'Upon the road and 20 miles out of the road if need shall require', and the provision of post horses 'for all that will ride with the letters' for 'single post pay', *viz.* 2½*d.* a mile and a groat to the guide at each stage.

Samuel Jude made vigorous efforts to defeat this attempt to put him out of business. In a petition of the following February the posts complain that 'the said Jude (as heretofore so now) labours to suppress your petitioners in this course also, and to that end he and his servants pulls down your petitioners' bills, and hath lately obtained your Lordships' Order to do as heretofore, without mentioning particulars, which if your Lordships permit will be the ruin and overthrow of your petitioners'. But a further Order of 24 February seems to have disposed of Jude,

[1] *Report of a committee of the Privy Council,* April, 1623. S.P. 14, CXLIII, 80. *Statement of Charges of necessity layd out and payd by former Paymasters,* 1623. S.P. 14, CXLIII, 54. *The humble petition of John Heydon Esquier and William Godson gentleman,* 23 Nov. 1623. S.P. 14, CLIV, 72.

and the scheme was a great success. Three years later it could be described as 'a service of great consequence tending to the public good of all his Majesty's subjects'.

Stanhope awoke to the fact that his posts had, by their own exertions and in spite of his indifference, put the posting system for the first time upon a profitable basis, and with characteristic thoughtfulness proceeded at once to 'raise the valuation of the Posts' places of the Western road from £20 anciently given to £100'. This was represented as a great injustice in 1633 by Edward and Joseph Hutchins who, upon the death of their father (the redoubtable Thomas), had expected to succeed him in his post-room at Crewkerne. But it is clear from their petition that they were ready enough to pay the £100 if they might have 'the benefit of the merchants' letters, which their father had'.[1] There could be no clearer evidence of the fact that under the new arrangements the posting business on the Plymouth road had become five times as profitable as it had been in the past.

The lesson to be drawn was obvious, and the only question that remained was who should be quick enough to draw it. If Stanhope had had his wits about him the honour, and the reward, of putting the whole posting system of the country upon a profitable basis might have been his. But he was not a man of business, and it was the wide-awake Postmaster for Foreign Parts, Thomas Witherings, who got in first with 'A Proposition for settling of Staffets or pacquet posts betwixt London and all parts of his Majesty's Dominions, for the carrying and recarrying of his Subjects' Letters. The cleere proffitt whereof to goe towards the payment of the Postmrs of the Roades of England. for which his Majestie is now chardged with £3400 per annum'. Witherings was appointed by Proclamation of 31 July 1635 to establish his proposed system on the roads to Edinburgh, Holyhead, Oxford, Norwich and Plymouth, with extensions to Bristol, Shrewsbury, Lincoln and other places. Thus the organization developed by the posts of the Plymouth road became the pattern for a national system, and survived as part of it. 'For the carriage of letters to Plymouth, Exeter and other places on that road' Witherings was specially instructed 'to take the like post that now is paid, as near as possibly he can'. The foundations laid by Thomas Hutchins were not to be disturbed.

[1] *Petition of Edward and Joseph Hutchins*, 1633. S.P. 16, CLXI, 27.

XVII

The Letter Post

It would hardly be possible to exaggerate the historical importance of this experiment by the posts of the Plymouth road. It ranks as the greatest social invention of a century which produced also the coffee house, the printed journal and the turnpike road. Like most great inventions it was simple, and at first not very spectacular. It meant that a shop keeper of Barnstaple, for instance, who hitherto had been obliged to wait three weeks or more for a reply from his supplier in London, could now get an answer in eleven days.[1] But this was only the first step. As soon as the post began to run more than once a week, he could get his answer in seven days or even less. By what must have seemed like a sudden shrinking of the map he found himself as closely in touch with London as a shop keeper of St. Alban's had been in Elizabeth's days. And this new facility, spreading along the five old post roads and branching out over the system of cross posts which Witherings undertook to set up, soon covered the whole country with a loose network of regular communications which mitigated the sense of isolation in which most country folk lived, and opened a new field for commercial enterprise. The delivery of goods of course remained as slow as ever: there could be no faster transport than the pack-horse until the railways came. But orders and advices and all the paper work of business began to move at such a rapid pace

[1] *H.M. Com. 9th Report*, Appendix, p. 214.

that it became possible, in the latter part of the century, to set up business in a remote country place without fear of perishing like a fly in treacle. One of the most eloquent complaints made in *The Compleat Tradesman* 1684, is of the inordinate increase of speculative shopkeeping, not only in the suburbs of London but throughout the country; 'for now' says the author, 'in every Countrey Village where is (or may be) not above ten houses, there is a Shop-keeper, and one that never served any apprenticeship to any Shop-keeping trade whatsoever; and many of those are not such that do deal only in Pins, or such small wares, but such that deal in as many substantial Commodities as any do that live in Cities and Market Towns, who have no less than 1000*l.* worth of Goods in their Shops, for which they pay not one farthing of any Tax at all, either Parochial or National. Certainly all men must needs apprehend that if this and Pedlars be suffered, that Cities and Market Towns must needs be impoverished; because there will be little occasion (I say) to bring the Countrey people to them; the which hath happened in very great measure already, for in some places there is not a fifth part of the money taken by the Shop-keepers as was formerly, and in many places not half'.

To the old fashioned tradesman this change in the map of trade was of course deplorable, but it was the expression of a profound change in the texture and spirit of country life.

The Elizabethan village had been, as far as legislation could make it, a self-sufficing and static unit, exhibiting that closed circuit of life which may be seen in a well balanced aquarium. Its fields, if open strip, were cultivated by ancient rule of thumb, without any restless attempt at improvement, or even at adequate drainage. If they were enclosed holdings they were often sheep walks or pastures that had not been 'swarded' within living memory, full of moss and ant hills and bosses of furze. Since the price of corn was steadily rising it would probably have paid the farmer to plough them up. But not he. Pasture had been good enough for his grandfather in the great wool days, and pasture was good enough for him. ' "What" saith he, "destroy my pasture, my sheep walkest, and beggar my land?" All the world shall not persuade him to that. "No" saith he, "I can raise a constant profit by my woole and lamb, my fat beef and mutton, at an easy quiet way unto my self and family, without much vexing and turmoiling".'[1] His farm thus lay spell bound under a cloud of golden memories. 'Whistness had taken possession of the woods; stilnes made aboad in the fields'; and the village folk went about their work in the foreground of this enchanted scene like people in a picture, unaware of any world outside it.

By the end of the seventeenth century this mood of anaerobic pastoral had almost gone. Old customs might still survive, and the round of rustic activities might appear to be much as it had been. But in almost every village now there were men and women who had had to fight or to suffer for a public cause, and in the process had attained a new mental horizon. 'Reader', says old Roger Crab, who had been left for dead at Nazeby, 'this is to let thee understand, when I was in my Earthly Garden a digging with my Spade, with my Face to the East side of the Garden, I saw into the Paradise of God from whence my Father Adam was cast forth'.[2] Even in those who were far from being visionaries the change was equally apparent. 'It seemeth marvellous to me', says Fuller in his *Mixt Contemplations*, 'that many Mechanicks (few able to read, and fewer to write their names) turning Souldiers and Captains in our Warrs, should be so soon and so much improved. They seeme to me to have commenced *per saltum* in their understandings. I profess, without flouting or flattering, I have much admired with what facility and fluentness, how pertinently and properly they have expressed themselves, in language which they were never born nor bred to, but have industriously acquired by conversing with their betters. . . . Not that I write this (God knoweth my heart) in disgrace of them, because they were bred in so mean callings, which are both honest in themselves and useful in the commonwealth; yea, I am so far from thinking ill of them for being bred in so poor trades, that I should think better of them for returning unto them again'.[3]

Fuller is thinking chiefly of town craftsmen, 'tailors, shoe makers, cobblers' and the like; but it was equally true of country workers. Agriculture itself was becoming a more intelligent

[1] W. Blith. *The English Improver Improved*, 1652, p. 74.
[2] Roger Crabb. *Dagons Downfall*, 1657, p. 20.
[3] Thomas Fuller. *Mixt Contemplations in Better Times*, 1660, xvii.

occupation. Much land was now farmed by men of education who had lost part of their estates during the civil war, and were managing the remnant themselves on what were thought to be scientific principles. Even the small freeholder or 'statesman' farmer, obstinate and pig headed as he might still be, was no longer wholly impervious to new ideas. He would tell you that an old pasture 'puts not that proofe into Cattel, nor scarce half as much, as it did at the first soarding'. If it is run over with a Flag grasse, or Anthills, Mossure or Wild Time' it ought to be denshired, or at least ploughed deep'; and he meant *deep*, for he had no patience with 'that ordinary way of Hilding Land as most do'. He had a great belief in deep drains, 'one spade's pitch or graft' below 'the spewing wet earth that breeds rush or mareblabb'. Run them through 'the coldest and most quealiest parts of thy land', and let them 'biggen and strengthen the further they run'. Mind you, 'it will ask paines, cost and hot water; yet faile not herein'. Note that for destroying anthills you need a spade 'a little more compasse or comming than your ordinary spades are'. And leave them hollow, so that the Turfe may have time 'to sodder and worke together, before the dry weather comes to parch it'. Plant your sets early, for delay 'will so backen them' that you may lose 'a full half year's growth'. He was not too fond of sycamores; they were apt to be 'Anusancies', for in Spring 'you shall find the seeds chitted up and down as thick as possible'. But whatever you choose to plant, protect the saplings 'untill they be rootened and stifned so strong that they will endure a beast rubbing upon them'. In everything that you do 'omnify God', and remember that an ingenious man is but 'a Midwife to deliver the Earth of it Throwes'.

To call him a scientific farmer would perhaps be, in Cleveland's phrase, 'to Knight a Mandrake'. But some slight whiff of the scientific preoccupations of his age had reached him by osmosis. He ripened his cheeses in his bedroom to secure an equable temperature; and he had once tried mulching some tulip bulbs with different coloured inks. It is true that 'it did not answer'; but it was a thing that his father would never have dreamt of, and it gave him a sense of being in the van of progress. Meanwhile the Government bounties on corn had enabled him to put by money. His wife was the sister of an impoverished gentleman, and his daughter was learning to play the virginals, 'a Courtlike breeding'.[1]

She too was a significant figure in the new picture. Adam Martindale, writing about 1685, could remember the time when freeholders' daughters in his native Lancashire 'were confined to their felts, petticoats and waistcoates, crosse handkerchiefs about their neckes, and white crosse clothes upon their heads, with coifes under them wrought with black silk or worsteed. 'Tis true the finest sort of them wore gold or silver lace upon their waistcoates, good silk laces (and store of them) about their petticoates, and bone laces or workes about their linnens. But the proudest of them (below the gentry) durst not have offered to weare an hood, or a scarfe, (which now every beggar's brat that can get them thinkes not above her) noe, nor so much as a gowne till her wedding day. And if any of them had transgressed these bounds, she would have been accounted an ambitious foole'.[2]

This business of the French hood, or *chaperon*, was a long established grievance. Even in Ireland, which lagged behind England in fashion, old gentlemen had been grumbling about it as early as 1619.

'Hee that would have come to a Lady in Ireland, but some five or six yeeres' sithence', says Barnaby Rich, 'and have asked her if shee would have had a *Shaparowne*, shee would have thought he had spoken bawdy, and would have wondred what hee had meant. They are now conversant to every Chamber-maide, and she that came lately out of a kitchen, if her Husband doth beare an office (how meane soever) if shee be not suted in her *Shaparowne*, in her loose hanging gowne, in her petticoates of sattin, yea and of velvet, that must be garded with silver or gold lace from the knee downe to the foote, her Husband may happen to heare of it, and (peradventure) to fare the worse till she be provided: for at every meale she will give him so many pout-pasties and carpe-pies, that shee will make him weary of his life'.[3]

[1] W. Blith. *The English Improver Improved*, 1652; *Blundell's Diary*, 1702–28. ed. Gibson, 1895; *Best's Farming Book* (Surtees Soc. 33); Henry Peacham *The Truth of our Times*, 1638. (p. 117. 'Of Clownes and rude behaviour'); Wye Saltonstall *Picturae Loquentes*, 1631. ('A Farmer's Daughter.)

[2] *The Life of Adam Martindale* (Chetham Soc.), p. 6.

[3] *The Irish Hubbub*, 1619.

But a girl now laughed at such scolding. She valued her French hood for the same reason that the ex-soldier valued the buff coat hanging behind his door, as a symbol of emancipation and the assertion of a claim to a better standard of life. Even the physical appearance of post-Restoration country towns and villages was beginning to reinforce the claim. Although the 'poore village' described by Saltonstall, with its wattle-and-daub walls and thatched or sodded roofs, was still to be seen in many places, there was a growing tendency to use better materials, and to pay more attention to the amenities. 'We may well admire', says the agriculturist Worlidge in 1681, 'at such as are not highly delighted at the prospect of most of our Country Villages, whose Beauty and Lustre daily encrease (where the Inhabitants are Industrious) and appear more and more neat, adorned and enriched, and in every part yield innumerable of pleasant and fruitful trees. Can there be a more ravishing and delightful object, than to behold the Towns Planted with Trees in even Lines before their doors, which skreen their Habitations from the Wind and Sun, where they may sit or walk under the dark shadow of the Woods and Groves?'[1]

To attribute all these complex changes to an improvement of communications would be absurd. But it may perhaps be said that in the chemistry of the process the newly invented Post had acted as a catalyst by establishing a regular traffic in news and ideas. In the old days the countryman famishing for news had had to go and fetch it. 'He delayes every passenger with inquiry of newes', says Thomas Adams in 1629, 'and because the Countrey cannot satiate him he travels every Terme to London for it, whence returning without his full loade, himselfe makes it up by the way. He buyes letters from the great citie with Capons; which hee weares out in three dayes, with perpetuall opening them to his companions'.[2] But now these news-letters could be had, by arrangement, at any post-house, and were to be seen at almost any village inn, where 'over a boull or Nogg' the local squire might be heard holding forth on their contents 'like a little Newsmonger'.[3]

[1] *Systema Agriculturae*, 1681. Preface.
[2] The Works of Thomas Adams. 1630, p. 472.
[3] *Remarks upon Remarques, or a vindication of the conversations of the Town* (anon.), 1673.

It was the social quite as much as the commercial effects of the Post that made it important. It meant not merely that the shop keeper could get his price list and place his orders, but that the Parson could get his Gazette, and that the Squire could hear what was being said in the London coffee houses before the talk was stale. This of course did not necessarily make anybody more intelligent. The great majority of country dwellers were no doubt as stupid as ever. But they had been provided with new ideas to be stupid with, and were in a position to share the stupidities of their betters. Thus though the social contrast between Town and Country remained, the insulation that separated them had begun to wear thin, and it is evident that Sir Roger de Coverly belongs to a much larger world than Justice Shallow. For one thing he is a Tory; and what is more, a critical reader of *Dyer's Newsletter*. Compared with a man at this impressive stage of social development Justice Shallow is a tadpole. And the essential difference between them is traceable at least in part to the fact that in 1629 a group of bilked and angry posts were permitted, as a favour, to carry an express packet of private letters from London to Plymouth, and from Plymouth to London, once a week.

XVIII

The Coach

THE coach heaves into view like a circus elephant and tries to steal the show. It was the latest attempt to solve a problem that had puzzled wainwrights for centuries, *viz.* how to design a vehicle that could move at a trot without jolting its occupants to pieces. It added nothing to the speed, and little, if anything, to the pleasure of travel; but it enabled the very old and the very young, the infirm and the timid or feckless, to travel without attendants. The coach made it possible to transport an invalid to Bath without troublesome and expensive negotiations for a horse litter, or to bring a schoolboy home for the holidays without sending a man and horses to fetch him. In such cases it was manifestly a convenience, and it was soon allowed to be a convenience in others. By means of the coach idle nobodies of moderate means were soon able to flock in large numbers to places like Bath and Tunbridge Wells and enjoy the sense of entering the World of Wit and Fashion. Beau Nash's empire was largely created and maintained by the coach.

But until nearly the end of the seventeenth century travel by coach was considered effeminate by gentlemen of the old school. They were fond of pointing out that 'in Sir Philip Sidney's time 'twas as much disgrace for a cavalier to be seen in London riding in a coach in the street as now 'twould be to be seen in a petticoate and Waistcote'.[1]

[1] Aubrey's *Brief Lives*, ed. Clark, 1898, II, 267.

Ralph Thoresby's father felt obliged to bring his son from Hull to York in a coach after his serious illness in 1678; but, says Ralph, 'it proved a mortification to us both, that he was as little able to endure the effeminacy of that way of travelling, as I was at present to ride on horseback'. The old man persuaded him to ride the last part of the journey from York to Leeds, 'weak and crazy' as he was.[1]

Attempts to apply the principle of a litter to the body of a wheeled vehicle had been made very early, and by the middle of the fourteenth century they had resulted in a clumsy thing called a 'chare', 'chariot' or ' whirlicote'. From an illumination in Cotton MS. (Claud. B. iv), and a partial description in *The Squire of Low Degree*,[2] the 'chare' seems to have been structurally nothing but a small waggon, but with carved and gilded standards from which a canopied nacelle was slung on ornamented chains. It was used chiefly as a conveyance for great ladies or great invalids, but also on occasions when some decorous haste might be required. The body of Richard II was displayed in Cheapside on a chare drawn by four horses, and attended by 'four knights all in black'. After two hours 'they drew the chare forward, and when the four knights that followed the chare afoot were without London, they leapt then on their horses, which were ready for them, and so they rode till they came to a village called Langley, a thirty mile from London, and there was this King Richard buried. God have mercy on his soul'.[3] Berners calls it a 'chare'; Higden a 'chariot'. Whatever its right name, it was evidently a vehicle in which an inconvenient royal corpse could be hustled handsomely but expeditiously into oblivion.

According to Stow these vehicles had already begun to fall into disuse because the side saddle had been made fashionable by Richard's Queen, Anne of Bohemia. She 'first brought hither the riding upon side saddles, and so was the riding in Whirlicotes and Chariots forsaken, except at coronations and such like spectacles'.[4] But it seems clear that this primitive type of coach, slung on chains, survived in less ornamental form until much later. In the early sixteenth century the Earl of Northumberland

[1] *Diary of Ralph Thoresby*, ed. Hunter, 1830, I, 28.
[2] G. Ellis. *Specimens of the Early English Poets* (1790), I, 339.
[3] Lord Berners. *Froissart's Chronicles*, Ch. CCXLV.
[4] John Stow. *A Survey of London*, ed. Morley, 1890, p. 110; and see Note 012.

still had a 'chariot' with 'VII Great Trotting horses'; but it was now used, not for conveying the ladies, but for sending most of 'the Chappel stuff' ahead of the main party when the household moved, presumably in order that the chapel might be ready for use upon his Lordship's arrival.[1]

A similar chariot was evidently among the effects of the second Earl of Cumberland in 1572:

> Itm. the old chariett with 2 pair of wheeles bound with iron, and cheynes belonging thereto. xxxs[2]

It seems probable that the vehicle 'with chains to stretch under the carriage' in which the carrier conveyed Höchstetter and his family from London to Keswick in 1571 was of the same ancient pedigree;[3] and perhaps the last glimpse we get of this old, indigenous type of coach is in the description of the celebrated 'GEE HO', which was still remembered by old people in Shrewsbury when Owen and Blakeway were collecting materials for their *History* of the town, published in 1825. It was described as 'a large leathern box, something like a coach, . . . hung upon chains in the middle of the waggon. People of bettermost class were thus separated from their inferiors. . . . It was drawn by eight horses, with two more to drag it through sloughs and up hills. Seven, eight and even nine days were sometimes consumed in the journey (to London). Such a conveyance existed in 1740, and perhaps earlier; and no other was known at Shrewsbury till 1750'.[4]

The description may help to explain some rather puzzling entries in early coach directories, e.g. 'the waggon or coach of Hatfield', 'the waggon or coach of Hertford', mentioned in Taylor's *Carrier's Cosmography* 1637; and 'the Coachwaggons' of Coventry, Grantham and other places, advertised in *The Present State of London* 1681. Were these coaches or waggons? Surely the answer is that they were 'GEE HOS': waggons with a slung compartment for first class passengers, and probably direct descendants of the clumsy 'chares' and 'chariots' of the fourteenth century. But the type of coach which took the road in Elizabeth's reign, and set an entirely new standard of English

[1] *Regulations and Establishment of the Household of . . . the Fifth Earl of Northumberland*, ed. T.P., 1770, p. 386.

[2] Inventory quoted in Whitaker's *History of Craven*, p. 238.

[3] W. G. Collingwood. *Elizabethan Keswick*, p. 142.

[4] Owen and Blakeway. *A History of Shrewsbury*, 1825, I, 513.

coach building, was the Pomeranian: beautifully timbered and decorated by expert German craftsmen, slung on leather braces (sometimes apparently, with spring shackles),[1] and although, no doubt, a heavy job when judged by later standards, light enough to be drawn quite adequately by two horses. In 1576 a coach of this kind could be bought in Pomerania and delivered in London, with a set of spare wheels, for £42;[2] but having been made for the German market, its roof would be found inconveniently low in England, where there was a fashion for wearing very tall, conical hats with plumes.[3] The coach would therefore have to be sent to the Queen's coach-maker in Smithfield to have its roof raised at a further cost of £8. 10*s.*, making the total just over £50. But this was only for the coach-work. The upholstery and trimming might cost two or three times as much as the coach itself. Lord Manners paid £122. 19*s.* 1*d.* for the orange-coloured leather, taffeta curtains, crimson velvet cushions, fringes and embroideries provided for his coach in 1599,[4] and there is no reason to suppose that such expenditure was exceptional. For the grand discovery had been made that, for a landed gentleman in a world of fixed rentals and constantly rising prices, a handsome coach was the cheapest way of keeping up appearances. Hitherto, when his Lady went visiting on horseback, she had had to be attended by a bevy of servants. 'She must have one to carry her cloake and Hood, least it raine, another her Fanne, if she use it not herselfe, another her box with Ruffes and other necessaries, another behinde whom her Mayde or Gentlewoman must ryde, and some must be loose to open Gates, and supply other services that may be occasioned'. All this had cost money in wages, board and liveries, to say nothing of the additional horse-keep and stabling. But now in a coach 'she with her Gentlewomen, Mayde and Children, and what necessaries they or any of them are to use, may be caryed and conveyed with smaller charge, less cost, and more credite, as it is accompted: for one or two men besides the Coachman are sufficient for a Gentlewoman or Lady of worthy parentage'.[5]

[1] 'A paire of springe trees' and 'a long spring brace' were provided for the coach of Lord Manners in 1598. *H.M. Com. Rutland*, IV, 420.

[2] See Note 013.

[3] See Note 014.

[4] *H.M. Com. Rutland*, IV, 421.

[5] *A Health to the Gentlemanly Profession of Serving men*, by W.W., 1598.

A coach was therefore not as expensive as it looked. It enabled the landed gentleman to cut down his establishment, close his country house for part of the year, and get rid of those 'twenty old fellows in blue coats and badges' (relics of his father's règime) who spent most of their time pestering the maids, and teaching the young son of the house how to drink a health and twang his glass in the buttery; while for the gentleman of more moderate means, who had no 'bluecoats' but sons and daughters to place in the world, a coach had the inestimable advantage that it gave him fair access to London—London, the great marriage-market, swarming with eligible young men and wealthy citizens' daughters.

True, London prices were high. But 'I persuade myself', says Edward Waterhourse, writing in 1665 but making a calculation which had often been made in Elizabeth's reign, that 'taking one time and thing with another, as we vulgarly say, a Family may live as handsomely and cheap in London as in any part of England; for though Rents are dear, and Rates upon Commodities and Estates higher than in any other part, yet is it ballanced by little Hospitality, Fewness of Servants, Variety of food of all natures haveable with money in an instant, and in what proportion Housekeepers please, and their Houses can spend'.[1] Thus even for a man of moderate means a coach might be a sound investment; and it had the further advantage that it helped to break the ice; for the coach was indirectly a leveller. As long as it was the distinguishing mark of a gentleman that he kept open house in the country, the London business-man could not compete. He had to mind his shop. But as soon as a gentleman became identifiable with a person who kept a handsome coach, a barrier was down. Any rich shopkeeper could buy a coach, and thus enable his wife and daughters to crash gates that had hitherto been barred against them.

Thus the craze for coaches which seemed, in the last years of Elizabeth's reign, to be turning London into a Nineveh of extravagance, was really promoted by thrift and maintained by hard-headed calculation. It was far too firmly rooted in the economic needs of the time to yield to sumptuary legislation. An Act submitted to the Lords in 1601 proposed that 'noone under the degree of a Knight, Privy Counsellor, Queen's

[1] E. Waterhouse. *The Gentleman's Monitor*, 1665, p. 297.

Counsel etc or paying £50 to the subsidy shall ride or travel in coaches under penalty of £5 for every offence, and no person shall let a coach, or coach horses, to any but those herein authorized to use them, upon pain of forfeiting the same'.[1] But it was precisely because many a gentleman was finding it difficult to pay his subsidy that he needed a coach to better his fortunes; and as for the coach-hire, it was common knowledge that some of the Lords who considered the measure were quietly reducing the cost of their coaches by hiring them out to contractors.[2] The proposed Act was a mere flourish of Mrs Partington's mop, and never had a second reading.

That the coach was used as a means of lavish, and sometimes excessive, display there can be no doubt. The monstrous over-elaboration of some of the Queen's coaches had set an example in this matter. But it was a moment in history when display was a necessary adjunct of civilized life and even an instrument of diplomacy. The courtier who sent his richly decorated coach to meet an incoming Ambassador was playing a real and indispensable part in international relations. And the beauty of it was that he could now send his coach instead of going himself. What mattered on these tedious occasions was that there should be a good turn-out of coaches belonging to Distinguished Persons: who might be sitting in them was of less importance. Indeed, it was on the whole desirable that some of them, at least, should be empty and available for members of the incoming Ambassador's suite. The use of coaches thus came to be governed by protocol, and the etiquette of the King's coach in particular became, in King James's reign, extremely intricate.

On very special occasions, when the negotiations related to Peace, Marriage or the Baptism of royal children, the King's coach might be sent to meet an Ambassador as far as Sittingbourne or even further. But the standing rule was that the Ambassador of a King—not, be it noted, of a republic or other ramshackle set-up—should have the King's barge from Gravesend to Tower Steps, and the King's coach from Tower Wharf to his lodging. On one painful occasion certain Commissioners of the States were duly met by Viscount Wimbledon at Tower Wharf with a handsome train of coaches, but the King's was

[1] *H.M. Com. 4th Report*, Appendix, 116.
[2] See Note 015.

not among them. This occasioned 'no small distaste', The resident Ambassador lodged a protest. The Master of Ceremonies hastened to explain that the mistake had arisen from 'the forgetfulness of my Lord Chamberlain's Gentleman of his horses'; though there is little doubt that the gaffe was his, and that he had thought the King's coach 'too high' (to use his own phrase) for these Commissioners of a democratic State. The matter was finally settled by smuggling them back 'by a private way about by London walls' to take a view of the Tower. They were then met again on Tower Wharf by Viscount Wimbledon with all the original coaches, but now with the King's, and also (for good measure) the Queen's, in addition; and in this amended glory they proceeded once more through the City to their lodging, and lived happily ever after.[1]

Meanwhile, beyond the verge of the Court, the London marriage-market was making fortunes for coach-builders.

> 'I shall have my coach and my coachman?'
> 'I' faith.'
> 'And two white Horses with black feathers to draw it?'
> 'Too.'
> 'A guarded Lackey to run before't, and pyed Liveries to come trashing after't?'
> 'Thou shalt, Moll.'
> 'And to let me have money in my purse to go whether I will?'
> 'All this.'
> 'Then come what so e're comes on't, wee'le bee made sure together before the Maydes o' the kitchen'.[2]

Even in this innocent world Etiquette sometimes reared its serpent head. The coachman of a Countess always drove bare headed, wet or fine. It was even said that bald headed men were preferred for such posts, as being more conspicuously uncovered. There was therefore a certain inducement for ambitious ladies of lower rank to contrive the liquidation of their coachmen's hats. The hired coachman in Jonson's *The New Inn* IV.2 enters hatless and explains:–

> 'The wind blew't off at Highgate, and my lady would not endure me light to take it up.'

[1] *Finetti Philoxenis*, 1656, p. 243. (Notes of ceremony made between 1612 and 1628 by Sir John Finett while Assistant Master of Ceremonies.)
[2] *The Puritane Widow* (1607), Act IV, sc. 1.

'That she might be taken for a countess?'
'Troth, like enough; she might be an overgrown duchess for aught I know.'

(A 'duchesse' was a large, insipid kind of peach that soon went sleepy.)

This of course is satire; but there is little doubt that such incidents did occur, and that a serious view could be taken of them. During the examination of Lord Chief Justice Coke in 1616 the Lord Treasurer 'told him that he had one thing more to let him know, which belonged to the Earle Marshall to take notice of; which was that his coachman used to ride Bare headed before him; which was more than anie wayes he could assume or challenge to himself: and required him to forbeare it for the future. To which the Lord Chief Justice answered, that his coachman did it only for his own ease, and not by his commandement'.[1]

Moll would have to think twice about hiding her coachman's hat, or she might have the Earl Marshal after her! But there! Behind two white horses with black plumes and a guarded Lackey running before them, even if she was not taken for a Countess she would certainly be taken for Somebody; and this was perhaps enough to go on with.

By 1619 the coachmakers' trade had become 'the most gainefullest about the towne', says Taylor, and the hackney coaches that they kept turning out had created such a traffic problem that the Common Council had to take action. One of the worst traffic blocks was near the Blackfriars theatre; for the coach was having its effect upon the drama. The ladies who went to see Shakespeare's earlier plays at the Globe must have gone by wherry or on horseback, and the heroines whom they favoured were venturesome young women who might have done the same thing: Viola, Rosalind, Portia. But the audience that crowded to the plays of Beaumont and Fletcher, Ford and Shirley, was largely composed of 'nice things' who had been wafted to the theatre in a coach, and the fashionable heroines now tend to be 'nice things' of the same sort, sentimental, pliable and neurotic. The coach had also affected Sunday observance. A carrier caught driving his waggon through the

[1] Ben Jonson. *The New Inn* (1629), Act IV, sc. 2; *Baker MS.*, quoted in Peck's *Desiderata Curiosa* (1779), p. 216.

streets on a Sunday was promptly arrested and fined. But a lady driving to Church in her coach raised a difficult question. Why should the compliment that was regularly paid to an Ambassador be denied to Almighty God? A lady of title could not be expected to trudge through the mud on foot. It was the distinguishing mark and manifest of her high estate that she never stooped to such antics. If therefore she were deprived of her coach she would be deprived of proper liberty to perform her religious duty.

'His Majesty little knows', says Barnaby Rich, 'what harme he doth to poore women when he makes them Ladies: Alas for pitty, a woman is no sooner Ladified but she hath lost the use of her legges for ever after; she is presently become so lame and decrepit that she cannot go to Church if she have not a Coach'.[1]

So Sunday coaching had to be winked at, and the rumble of wheels on a Sunday morning became so loud that it sometimes drowned the preacher's voice; and they were obliged to 'set up a Crosse post in Cheapside on Sundaies near Wood Street end, which makes the Coaches rattle and rumble on th' other side of the way, further from the Church and from hindering of their hearing'.[2]

This sudden multiplication of wheels had compelled a more serious attention to the state of the roads. During Elizabeth's reign there had been no less than nineteen enactments for the improvement of roads in and about the city, and by 1617, according to Fynes Moryson, the roads 'one or two daies any way from London' were 'sandy and very faire, and continually kept so by labour of hands'. Pleasure-coaching had thus become possible. The traffic welled out into the country adjoining, and Taylor (who hated coaches because they were putting the watermen out of business) sourly notes the new fashion among prosperous shop-keepers 'to be coach'd to S't Alban's, Burntwood, Hockley-in-the-Hole, Croydon, Windsor, Uxbridge and many other places, like wilde Haggards prancing up and downe; that what they get by cheating, swearing and lying at home, they spend in riot, whoring and drunkennes abroad'.

But it will be noted that all these places are within thirty-five miles of London. Outside that area in the untamed country none

[1] Barnaby Rich. *The Irish Hubbub*, 1619.
[2] John Taylor's *Works*, 1630, p. 239.

coached for pleasure, and few for any reason except inability to mount a horse. The geographical division was so sharp that a distinction begins to be made between the 'caroche', the pleasure vehicle used within this magic circle, and the 'coach' which penetrated the wilderness beyond. A wealthy suitor is now one who keeps 'a coach for country and caroche for town'.[1]

In Dekker's *Seven Deadly Sins of London* Lying, upon his arrival from the country, leaves his chariot to be dismantled outside Moorgate, walks into Coleman Street, and is promptly furnished by the welcoming hackneymen with his 'caroache'. Although the caroche was not made with a folding roof until 1625,[2] it was evidently, like the later calèche, an open sort of carriage, used by people who wished to be seen and admired. It was while driving in his 'carrosse' over Holborn Bridge in 1612, 'with his great lechugador (ruff) about his neck and coming upon his elbow', that the Spanish Ambassador had his hat snatched from his head by 'a fellow on horseback'.[3] The coach, on the contrary, was much used by people who, for some reason, did not wish to be seen. This was the main objection urged against it in the proposed Act of 1601. 'Evil disposed persons, who dare not shew themselves openly for fear of correction, shadow and securely convey themselves in coaches, and cannot be discerned from persons of honour'. The explanation is that it was an all-weather vehicle, equipped with heavy curtains or screens against the rain, and in spite of the frivolous or scandalous uses to which it might be put, designed for the serious business of travelling.

And in regions remote from London a very serious business it was. Sir Ralph Sadler found it quite impossible to convey the Queen of Scots by coach from Wingfield to Tutbury without first 'causing bridges to be made to avoid many evill passages', and even then the journey of twenty odd miles took two days. One of Queen Elizabeth's journeys is described as 'marvellous for speed and expedition' because she only had to leave the coach once, 'while the hinds and folk of a base sort lifted it on with their poles.' Lady Clifford, approaching Manchester over the moors in 1616, found the 'wayes so dangerous the horses

[1] *Green's Tu Quoque*, Dodsely's *Old Plays* (1744), III, 18.
[2] Note 016.
[3] Note 017.

were fain to be taken out of the coach to be lifted down the hills'; and Prince George of Denmark, driving from London to Petworth in 1703, sat in his coach without food for fourteen hours, of which the last six were spent in covering nine miles. 'We were thrown but once indeed', says one of his suite, 'but would have suffered very often if the nimble boors of Sussex had not poised and supported it with their shoulders from Godalmin almost to Petworth'.[1]

For bulldozing like this a coach had to be stoutly built. It can be calculated from carriers' charges in the Naworth accounts for bringing coach wheels from Newcastle, that each fore wheel of Lord Howard's coach[2] in 1633 weighed about 100 lb., and each hind wheel about 200 lb. But this was probably before the 'strakes' had been put on by the Naworth blacksmith. The strakes were strips of iron plate, or perhaps of channel iron, forged to the contour of the wheel, and fixed to the felloes in such a way as to bridge the joints between them. Five and a half stone of iron were allowed for 'two streikes to the coach' (meaning presumably the strakes for two wheels), so that each wheel must have carried about 38 lb. weight of iron.

A coach built to this margin of strength must have been very different from an elegant town caroche, with its wheels bound with felt to diminish rattle.[3] It differed also in its slinging. If the braces of a coach were tight they transmitted the jolts of a cobbled surface almost as badly as if it were not slung at all. The London coaches were therefore slung loosely. But on a heavily rutted country road a loosely slung coach developed a dangerous swing which threatened to overturn it. Travelling coaches were therefore tightly braced, and the travellers had to forgo almost all the advantages of the slinging for the sake of remaining upright.[4] The normal load was six persons; but in some coaches two more could be carried, sitting one in each doorway, and protected from the weather by what was called a 'boot': a semi circular hoop carrying an apron of leather or black cloth, which could be drawn down and fastened. Here sat

[1] Sadler, III, 262; S. Smiles *Life of Thomas Telford*, 1867; *The Diary of the Lady Ann Clifford* (1923), p. 21; *Annals of Queen Anne*, 1704, Vol. II. Appendix.

[2] Note 018.

[3] Note 019.

[4] Ned Ward. *London Spy*, 1703, quoted by R. Strauss in *Carriages and Coaches* (1912), p. 164.

the shivering Gentlewoman or Chambermaid, watching the world crawl by, and keeping the draught off her mistress. What happened to her when the coach went over on her side 'may admit of a wide solution'. For some reason the right, or offside, boot was considered more eligible than the other, and was reserved for the Lady's Gentlewoman, while the Chambermaid sat on the left.[1] I can only suppose that since the edges of an unmade road were usually softer and more treacherous than the middle, a coach following our English rule of the road more often overturned on its left side than on its right. After a normal collapse, therefore, the Gentlewoman would be found on top of, and not under, the Chambermaid, and her natural superiority would thus be maintained. Fortunately there was no broken glass to worry about. The first glass windows were fitted to the Duke of York's coach in 1665, and even after they had become common they were regularly replaced by canvas screens for a country journey.[2] In wet weather, therefore, the travellers must have lurched along in a tawny twilight, 'telling sad stories of the deaths of kings'. Wise people carried 'blankets, Linning, Neats Tongues, claret &c',[3] and only the careless forgot tools with which 'to break hedges', and a pistol to point—(or, on second thoughts, perhaps not to point)—at highwaymen. Luggage could be carried in the coachman's box and on a sort of footboard between the rear standards.

The number of horses varied. The earliest coaches had been drawn by two, and it seems to have been some time before anyone tried to cut a special dash by using four. In this connexion a curious point is raised by Marlowe's *Tamburlaine*, 1588. In Act V, sc. 1, of the second part Tamburlaine has four perfectly good captive kings whom he thinks of harnessing to his chariot, and if ever there was an occasion for cutting a dash, this was indubitably it. But although four horse coach teams had by then been in use for ten years or more,[4] he harnesses only two.

The reason is probably theatrical. In the early coaches the coachman sat, not on the slung portion of the vehicle, but on a

[1] Note 020.
[2] Note 021.
[3] *Papers of Thomas Woodcock* (ed. Moore Smith), p. 66.
[4] See Note 013.

bench or box fixed between the fore standards. This low position no doubt saved his face from being slashed by overhanging branches in a lane, but made four-in-hand driving impossible, and when more than two horses were used the leaders had to be controlled by a mounted groom or postilion. Hence if Tamburlaine had harnessed all four captives, one of his leading Kings (if verisimilitude was to be maintained) would have had to carry a rider pic-a-back, and the scene, which is grotesque enough already, would infallibly have been whooped and whistled into farce. Four horses were always allowed in Finett's time for the coaches supplied to foreign Ambassadors (except when someone had to be snubbed), and four horse teams usually (though not always) draw the chariots described in fiction and poetry of the period.

The first person to use a six-horse team in London was the Duke of Buckingham in 1619, and it is said to have infuriated the old Earl of Northumberland so much that he instantly set up a team of eight 'with which he rode through the City of London to the Bath, to the vulgar talk and admiration'.[1] But Buckingham's team only caused a stir because it was used in London. For a coach ploughing its way through deep country roads four horses, even if primed with shots of 'butter and ale',[2] might not be sufficient, as every long-distance carrier knew. The carriers had been forbidden by a fatuous proclamation of 1618, to use waggons at all, or to harness more than five horses in their carts; but they were continually being presented for using waggons with six, eight and even, in a desperate place like Lob Lane near Oxford,[3] as many as twelve horses. Their waggons were, of course, heavier than any coach, but in places where a waggon needed twelve horses a coach might well need six, and six became, in fact, the accepted coach-team in the later seventeenth century.

The horses most sought after for coach-teams were dappled Flanders mares, of which a pair could be bought in 1608 for £47.[4] But on most country estates where the master of the house had been talked into buying a coach, the farm horses were

[1] Arthur Wilson. *The Life and Reign of King James the first*, 1653, p. 130.
[2] *H.M. Com. Middleton*, pp. 431, 436.
[3] *Reportes del Cases in Camera Stellata*, ed. Baildon, and see Note 023.
[4] *H.M. Com. Hastings*, I, 373.

used when they could be spared from honest work. 'There is no possibility of my coming', writes Frances Russell to her husband in 1663, 'the horses are at plough'.[1] Since many country gentlemen shared the widely held opinion that to ride in a coach was unmanly, their coaches were hardly ever used, at all events in winter, except to take the ladies to Church, and to keep an expensive team especially for the purpose would have been, they felt, ridiculous. Defoe had seen a great lady in Sussex drawn to Church in her coach by a team of six oxen. And why not, a' God's name? What woman of sense would keep Flanders mares in such 'a heap of Dirt' as Sussex?[2]

These impediments, physical and social, inevitably limited the speed at which a country coach could move. In the London district it is probable that the coaches went pretty fast, and certain that they went as fast as they could. The Frenchman who observed in 1700 that 'All Englishman ride so fast upon the Road that you would swear there were some Enemy in the Arrière; and all the Coaches in London seem to drive for Midwives',[3] was describing a national characteristic which had been noted by Howell in 1642[4] and by Fynes Moryson in 1617 in almost the same words. England had long been 'the Hell of Horses', and the poor brutes had not escaped their Hell by drawing in smart harness. A pamphleteer describes a coach 'that scudded through London' during the plague of 1603, 'hung with Rue from the top to the toe of the Boote, to keepe the leather and the nayles from onfection', and with 'the very nosthril of the Coach-horses stopt with hearb-grace . . . Thus they ran through Cornhill just in the middle of the street, with such a violent Trample as if the Divell had been Coachman'.[5] This was a moment of panic; but speed was a topic of interest in London at any time.

'How is thy driving, Tom?' says a character in *The New Inn* to Tom Trundle, the coachman, 'Good as it was?'

TOM. It serves my Lady and our officer Prue.
Twelve miles an hour. Tom has the old Trundle yet.

[1] *H.M. Com. Russell* (1663).
[2] Defoe. *A Tour through Great Britain*, 1724; and see Note 022.
[3] *A Character of England*, Harleian Miscellany, III, 33.
[4] James Howell. *Instructions for Forraine Travell*, 1642 (Arber's reprint, p. 69).
[5] *The Meeting of Gallants at an Ordinary*, 1604 (Percy Soc. reprint, V, 13).

This is absurd if he is claiming it as his average; but it is likely enough that on one of the good roads near London coachmen sometimes touched that speed. A better idea of their average may perhaps be drawn from Lord Clarendon's letter, arranging to dine with a friend at Gorhambury, near St. Albans, twenty-three miles from London. 'Be sure we have oysters enough on Friday by twelve of the clocke, for I suppose being in a coach by eight will bring us to you by that hour';[1] i.e. he expects to do six miles an hour. This, it is true, was in 1665; but the St. Albans road was one of those over which Taylor had seen coach-parties of shopkeepers 'prancing up and downe' in 1619.

All this 'speeding', however, was confined to the London area. In the remoter parts of the country nobody talked about miles per hour. Coach-journeys were so dreary and exhausting that travellers were thankful to move by short stages, and to reckon their progress in days. If a coach did twenty-five miles in a day they were well enough pleased; if it did as much as forty, they were astonished, and worn out. The average, as far as I have been able to compute it, was just over twenty-nine miles, which, if we could assume an eight-hours day, would mean about 3½ miles an hour: somewhat faster than a carrier's waggon, but probably not as fast as a pack-train or a footpost.

It seems clear, then, that any attempt to describe the effect of the coach upon English society before 1650 must begin with a sharp distinction between the area within thirty miles of London and the rest of the country. In London and its environs the coach had greatly increased amenities, and by weakening class-distinctions had done something to create a more homogeneous society. It had enabled the bored citizen to get out into the country, and the no less bored gentleman to get out of the country into the town. It had provided the means by which foreign Ambassadors could approach with convenient decorum from Dover, and with the same convenient decorum recede towards Dover again. It had, in short, contributed much to the variety, fun and brilliance of the social scene. But in the cledgy wilderness beyond this charmed circle the coach had as yet made no real difference to communications, and except that it had enabled a few country ladies to get to Church dry, and so sit through long sermons without catching cold, it had contributed

[1] *H.M. Com. Verulam*, p. 66.

little to amenities. It might on occasion be used for a picnic. Taylor describes a picnic at Wharncliffe in 1639 to which Lady Wortley and her daughter were conveyed in a coach over three miles of 'rocks and cloud kissing mountains';[1] and in 1654 we are told of a young lady, on holiday in the country, who resolves 'to keep the coach' (sent by her brother to bring her back to London) 'in the country a week or ten days, to ride about and take leave of her friends ere she comes; and besides, the coachman hath an excellent faculty in catching of partridges (a sport she delights in) and she will recreate herself that way, and make some partridge pies to bring up with her'.[2] But this high handed treatment of the family Rolls Royce gives a false picture of country coaching. The young lady was evidently using a smart town caroche to dazzle country cousins, whose idea of a coach was derived from some ponderous juggernaut like Lord Howard's. For most of the year a country gentleman's coach slumbered in his coach house like some prehistoric monster, an object of awe to peeping villagers; and it was only gradually that its possibilities as a means of public transport were generally recognized.

[1] *Part of this Summer's Travels*, 1639.

[2] Letter of William Dobbins to John Percivale in *H.M. Com. Egmont*, I (pt. 2), p. 559.

XIX

Stage Coaches

THIS is clearly reflected in such records as have survived of the early stage coaches. The earliest recorded (by Taylor in his *Carriers Cosmography*, 1637) all with one exception plied from places within thirty miles of London: St. Albans (21), Hertford (24) and Hatfield (21). The exception is Cambridge (54), which had had a coach since 1629 that covered the distance in two days. It is not until 1645 (in *The Traveller's Director*) that coaches are noted as coming in from places as far off as Stamford (85) and Newark (125), and not until 1655–7 that we hear of coaches from places as remote as Exeter (170), Chester (182), York (196) and Newcastle (274). By this time there were coaches also from Southampton (77), Aylesbury (40) and Winchester (65), and after 1657 the number must have increased rapidly. In de Laune's *Present State of London* 1681 coaches are noted as coming to London from 88 towns, and in The *Traveller's and Chapman's Instructor* 1705, from 180.

A few of these public vehicles (De Laune mentions seven), were 'coach-waggons' of the 'Gee-ho' type which might claim to be coaches carrying some 'outside' passengers; though a truer description would probably be that they were passenger-waggons which carried a few 'inside' passengers in a special compartment. But the great majority were simply heavy travelling coaches of the kind already described, slung on braces without springs, and carrying only six persons. This made it easy for a selfish or fidgety traveller of means to book the whole coach, and leave other would-be passengers stranded. Madam Freke of Billney regularly booked the whole of the London coach from Lynn when she was not using her own, and it seems to have been a common practice.[1]

In describing it as selfish it is only fair to remember that coach-journeys were long, and that to be boxed up at such close quarters with some thoroughly uncongenial stranger for several days on end might be a sore trial.

'Friend, friend', says the Quaker to the raffish recruiting-officer in Steel's famous *Spectator*, 'we have hired this coach in partnership with thee to carry us to the great City; we cannot go any other way. This worthy mother must hear thee if thou wilt needs utter thy follies; we cannot help it, friend, I say: if thou wilt, we must hear thee; but if thou wert a man of understanding, thou would'st not take advantage of thy courageous countenance to abash us children of peace. Thou art, thou sayest, a soldier; give quarter to us who cannot resist thee. . . . To speak indiscreetly what we are obliged to hear by being hasped up with thee in this publick vehicle, is in some degree assaulting on the high road'. If every coach had carried such an admirable Quaker there would have been less temptation to book all the seats. Marmaduke Rawdon, having booked the whole of the Exeter-London coach in this way in 1655, found that he had upset the plans of a young gentlewoman who 'had come from Plymouth thinking to have gone to London that week', and was kind enough to take her in. But if she had been a less agreeable proposition as a travelling companion she would probably have had to spend another week in Exeter.[2]

To make sure of a place it was advisable to book a seat some days beforehand, or, perhaps, to catch the coachman on his outward journey, and explain by means of a silver diagram that you wished to be picked up on his return.[3]

The average speed of these public coaches was practically the same as that of a private coach, *viz.* thirty miles a day; and since most of them were travelling over main roads which, since the passing of an Ordinance of 1654, were receiving some

[1] *Mrs Elizabeth Freke her Diary*, ed. Mary Carbery, 1913, p. 43.
[2] *Life of Marmaduke Rawdon* (Camden Society), p. 70.
[3] *H.M. Com. Marquis of Bath*, II, 172.

attention from the Surveyors, they could generally manage with four horses. But from time to time attempts were made, by using six horses and arranging relays, to maintain a 'Flying Coach' which would cover more than fifty miles in a day. There were Flying Coaches of this kind between London and Chester (1657), Oxford (1669), Cambridge (1671), Worcester (1681), and no doubt other places. But the results were obtained, not really by going much faster, but by starting extremely early in the morning and going on for '12 hours', according to the advertisements, but actually for thirteen or fourteen. Ralph Thoresby, going to Cambridge by the one-day coach in 1714, notes in his Diary, 'After a weary night, rose by three; walked to Bishopsgate to take coach for Cambridge, was in time'; and Ambrose Bonwick, taking the same coach in the reverse direction, 'got up by three o'the'clock, and was not in London till past seven, and by that means caught some cold, which turned afterwards to an ague'. Passengers by the two-day coach from Bristol to London about 1700 started at 2 a.m.[1]

The dreariness of these early starts is well conveyed by a letter of 1676, dated 14 December. Charles Hatton had received instructions at eleven o'clock at night that a certain Mademoiselle la Chappel (presumably a lady's maid) lodging in White Hart Yard, was to be sent down to Northampton by the coach next morning. 'It was too late then', he writes, 'to advertise her, or take a place in the coach. But this morning, betwixt three and four of the clocke, I got up and was to go to White Hart Yard, in Drury Lane'. It was foggy, and he lost his way; but having got directions by knocking up a householder and pretending to be one of 'Lord Craven's fire-spies', he at last found the lady's lodging.

'Mad la Chappel would very desirously have deferred going down till the next opportunity of the coach, which I thought might have been displeasing to your Lordshippe, and I fully satisfyed her that it was absolutely necessary she should goe this day, for, should it thaw, perhapps the coach might not be able to passe of a weeke, or ten dayes.

'And when I had prevayled with her to resolve to goe as this day, I went to Smithfield, and it was but five of the clocke when

[1] *The Diary of Ralph Thoresby*, ed. Hunter, 1830, II, p. 229. *The Life of Ambrose Bonwick*, Latimer. *Annals of Bristol* (Eighteenth Century), p. 22.

I got thither; and when I had taken a place in the coach, I went to fetch Mad[ll], and, with an addresse to Mr Ebriel', (a saddler in Northampton who received packets for the Hatton family) 'I recommended her to the care of the passengers, and saw her trunke delivered to the carrier. I gave her 20 shillings in money, pay'd fivteene shillings for her passage, and for coach hire, porter, and breakfast I pay'd 4 sh 6d more'.[1] It was with these preliminaries that the poor Mademoiselle faced a two days' journey, among English strangers, and over frozen roads. The one alleviating circumstance must have been that she had had her breakfast. Among the disadvantages of the coach one of the most serious was that it offered a particularly attractive target for the solitary highwayman. His victims were well-to-do people, numbed with fatigue, bunched together, and easily covered by a single pistol. He could therefore work without confederates, develop a personal touch, and end life as a celebrated character. If there ever was a 'Golden Age' for highwaymen it was at this moment when coaches had become common, and pistols still had to be primed with a powder-horn before they would fire. In a sudden encounter a great advantage always lay with the man who had primed his the moment before. If an efficient percussion cap had been on the market the situation would have been different, and we should have heard less about impudent bullies like du Val. But this useful pestifuge was not invented until 1803. For more than a century every traveller by coach had to accept the fact that if they ran into trouble, and shooting started, the odds would be against him more or less heavily, according to the state of the weather.

It appears from one of Walter Pope's anecdotes about the quaint scholar, Isaac Barrow, that travellers sometimes insured each other against robbery.

'We were once going from Salisbury to London, he in the Coach with the Bishop, and I on Horseback. As he was entring the Coach, I perceivd his Pockets strutting out near half a Foot, and said to him "What have you got in your Pockets?"

'He replied "Sermons".

' "Sermons", said I, "give them me; my Boy shall carry them in his Portmanteau, and ease you of that luggage".

' "But," said he, "suppose your Boy should be robbd".

[1] *The Hatton Correspondence*. (Camden Society), I, p. 141.

' "That's pleasant!" said I, "Do you think there are Parsons Padding upon the Road for Sermons?"

' "Why, what have you?" said he, "It may be five or six guineas. I hold my Sermons at a greater rate; they cost me much pain and time".

' "Well then", said I, "if you'll insure my five or six Guineas against Lay Padders, I'll secure your bundle of Sermons against Ecclesiastical Highwaymen" '.

'This was agreed; he emptied his Pockets, and filled my Portmanteau with Divinity; and we had the good fortune to come safe to our Journey's end without meeting either sort of the Padders forementioned, and to bring both our Treasures to London'.[1]

Most coach journeys no doubt ended in this quiet and satisfactory way. But the discomfort and slow inefficiency of the early stage coaches were such as to make one wonder how they ever gained the favour of the public. They offered, however, certain advantages that outweighed their defects. Hitherto it had been impossible to transport old people or invalids or children without the cost and trouble of making special arrangements; and there were many others who, while not falling precisely within these catagories, were to all intents and purposes equally immobile: the gouty man who could not pull on a riding boot, the short sighted man who could not see well enough to guide his horse, and the stout or pregnant woman who dared not risk a fall. All these now travelled by coach as freely and safely as anybody, and constituted a new travelling public. But the great recommendation of the coach was that it was cheap: not indeed as cheap as the carrier's humble waggon, but for people of condition much the cheapest means of travel yet available.

Mlle. la Chappel's fare to Northampton was 15*s*. If she had been sent with a servant on hired hacks the horse hire (at 'journey' rate) would have been 22*s*., and if she had ridden post her fare would have been 40*s*. 7*d*. She might perhaps have ridden on a pillion behind the servant for single horse hire at 11*s*.; but there would still have been the stable charges and the man's board and lodging to be reckoned. For a lady there was certainly no cheaper means of travel than by coach. It may be true, as Cresset seems to think, that a man riding alone on a hired hack,

[1] *The Life of Seth, Lord Bishop of Salisbury*, by Dr. Walter Pope, 1697, Ch. xx.

and carrying his cloak bag on its crupper, could travel more cheaply.[1] His horse hire to Exeter, for instance, at the journey rate would probably have been 27*s*. 6*d*., and the summer coach fare in 1673 was £2. But for a long ride like this the traveller needed some special equipment. He had to have proper riding boots, thick 'vamps' or bootsocks made of baize or some such material, and an enormous coat or cloak, preferably with a tippet, and certainly with skirts long enough to keep the rain out of his boot tops. Even then, in wet and blustery weather his boots might fill with water and become so sodden that he would feel obliged to buy a new pair before the end of his journey.

'If your sonne and I', writes Philip Gawdy to his brother in October 1605, 'had not provyded our selves of new boots at Bury, I thinke we had got bothe our deathes before we had comme at London'. On a long journey Lord Howard of Naworth used to treat himself to two or three pairs.[2] There was the further consideration that a man travelling alone paid the full price for his meals on the way, whereas coach passengers, as Cresset notes, 'when they come to their inn, club together for a dish or two of meat, and having no servants with them, spend not above twelvepence or sixteen pence at a place'.[3]

By the time he had paid this difference on his meals, settled his stable charges, and perhaps bought a new pair of riding boots for 8*s*. or so, a rider's travelling expenses might not be far short of the coach fare; and the advantage, which the coach offered, of being set down at his destination dry, unmuddied and in his ordinary clothes might be well worth the difference.

Certainly Englishmen of Cresset's generation had come to think so, and were showing in the most convincing manner by ceasing to keep horses of their own. This was especially noticeable in the London area. In 1673, when Cresset wrote, coaches were running daily 'to almost every town' within twenty or thirty miles of London, and return coaches to places within ten miles, 'wherein passengers are carried at such low rates, that most persons in and about London, and in Middlesex, Essex,

[1] *The Grand Concern of England Explained*, 1673 (Harl. Misc., viii).

[2] *Letters of Philip Gawdy* (Roxb. Club), p. 160; *Household Books of Lord William Howard* (Surtees 68), p. 202. In 1618 a pair of riding boots cost 8*s*. See *The Chambers Family of Raby Cote* in *Cumberland and Westmoreland Antiquarian Society*, New Series 1, 208.

[3] *The Grand Concern of England Explained.*

Kent and Surrey gentlemen, marchants and other traders that have occasion to ride, do make use of them; some to keep fairs and markets, others to visit friends, and to and from their country houses, and about other business; who before these coaches did set up, kept a horse or two of their own, and now have given over keeping of the same. So that, by computation, there are not so many horses by ten thousand kept now in these parts, as there were before stage coaches set up'.

It was a great change in the Englishman's way of life. There had been a time, within living memory, when the smart young man about town had kept all his appointments on horseback.

> FAUSTUS, not Lord nor Knight, nor wise, nor old
> To every place about the towne doth ride;
> He rides into the fieldes, Playes to behold,
> He rides to take boate at the Water side,
> He rides to Powles, he rides to the ordinary,
> He rides. . . .[1]

But those days were over. Faustus now took what we can recognize as a cab, and, for longer excursions, something indistinguishable from a 'bus.

But it would be stupid to attribute the success of the coach wholly to the fact that it was convenient and cheap. The truth is that it was a kind of miracle. It costs us now some effort to remember that at the time when those long waggons and coaches began to appear on our roads, the great majority of Englishmen had never ridden in a wheeled vehicle at all, and the great majority of Scots had never even seen one. This was quaintly revealed by the behaviour of the gillies and servants who attended the Scots Lord to England in King James's train. They must have been, for the most part, hardy and active men who could trot all day at theer masters' stirrups. But when the carts were requisitioned for moving the Court into Wiltshire, to escape the plague of 1603, the Yeoman Cart-Taker was infuriated to see that these able-bodied fellows were 'loading the carts with half-lodes of stuff' and piling in themselves. 'There was sometimes 16 great bodies of men and women upon one cart', he says indignantly.[2] He supposed that it must be because they

[1] *Epigrammes*, 1590, by Sir John Davies.

[2] From a tract by Robert Fletcher, printed in *H.M. Com. 5th Report*, appendix p. 407.

knew 'no facion but their own'. But in this he was certainly mistaken. This was not the fashion of Scotland: these were people who had been on foot all their lives, enjoying the strange and intoxicating experience of a lift.

In England wheels were less wonderful; but some degree of the same enchantment must have been felt by a generation which had never known what it was to move without some exercise of skill and strength. Even on the quietest carrier's hack a man had to make a hundred petty decisions and put forth a hundred petty efforts in every mile that he travelled. But here was a leathern Ark in which he could move over hundreds of painful miles to Exeter or Chester or Newcastle, without making a single decision or doing a single thing. It offered the first respite he had ever known from those incessant calls upon his initiative made by every moment of his waking life. It was, in fact, his first taste of what we now call mechanization; and the crowds who rumbled out of London in those early coaches were beginning the great trek that has gone on ever since, from a world in which a man did things for himself towards a world in which he has things done for him.

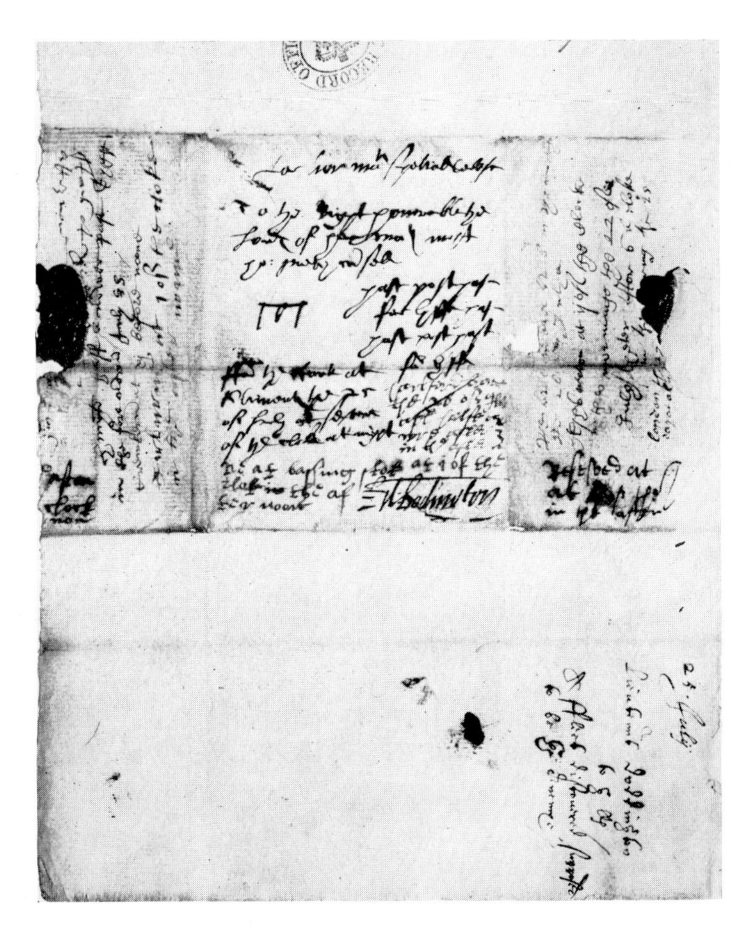

FOR HER MA's SPECIALL CERVISE

TO THE RIGHT HONOURABLE THE
LORDS OF HER MA's MOST
HO: PRIVEY COSELL

hast post hast
for lyff hast
hast post hast
for lyff

FFROM THE WORK AT PLIMOUTH THE 25 OF JULY AT SEVEN OF THE CLOCK AT NYGHT

Hartford Bridge
the x6 of July
at halfe an
hour after 3
in the after n

Re at Bassing stoke at 1 of the
clock in the af
ter noon

E. DODINGTON

the mrqt Hall Andover past Eyght
in the fore noon July 8s
Crewkerne at xj before noone
Xirburne at 1 of the cloke
in the after noone.

Stains at VII
afternone

Shafton
clock
non

Rec at Honiton at 8 in the morning
the 26 of July
Eshburton at ij of the clock
in the morning the 22 of
July. Exeter after 6 a cloke
in the morning Jul 25
London the 27
day at al

Reseyved at
at 4 of the
in the after

1. An urgent letter from Lieutenant Dodington to the Privy Council, July 25, 1599. (See Note 025)

2. A "shod" harvest cart on a steep hill

3. A loaded waggon in a very awkward lane, by W. Faithome

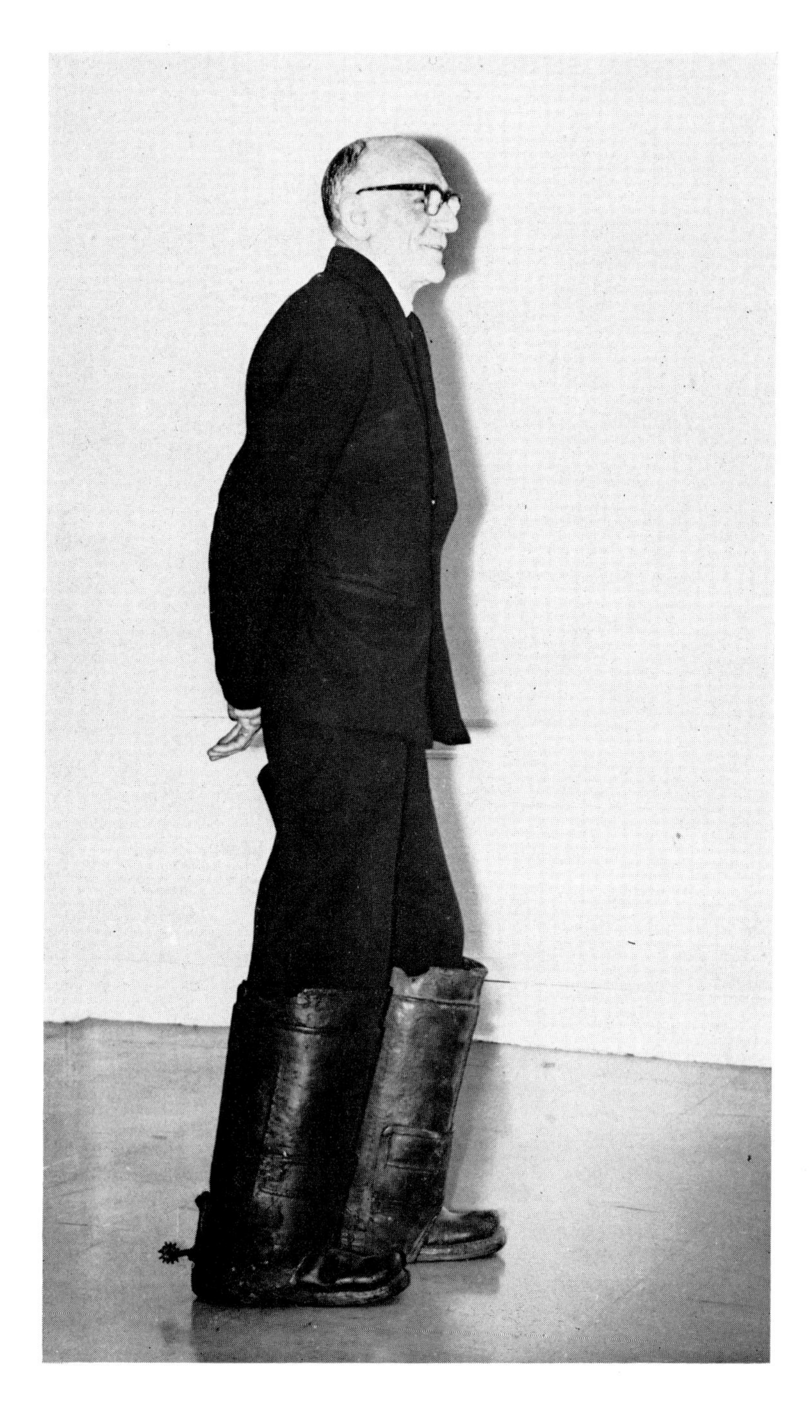

4. Riding Boots of a Postboy, 1650. (See Note 026)

5. Title page of John Ogilby's *Britannia*, Vol. 1. 1675 (British Museum)

COACH and SEDAN,

Pleaſantly Diſputing for Place and Precedence;

The *Brewers-Cart* being Moderator.

Spectatum admiſſi, riſum teneatis amici?

LONDON:
Printed by *Robert Raworth*, for *Iohn Crowch*; and are to be ſold by *Edmund Paxton*, dwelling at *Pauls* chayne, neere Doctors-Commons. 1636.

6. Title page of *Coach and Sedan pleasantly disputing* 1636, by Henry Peacham

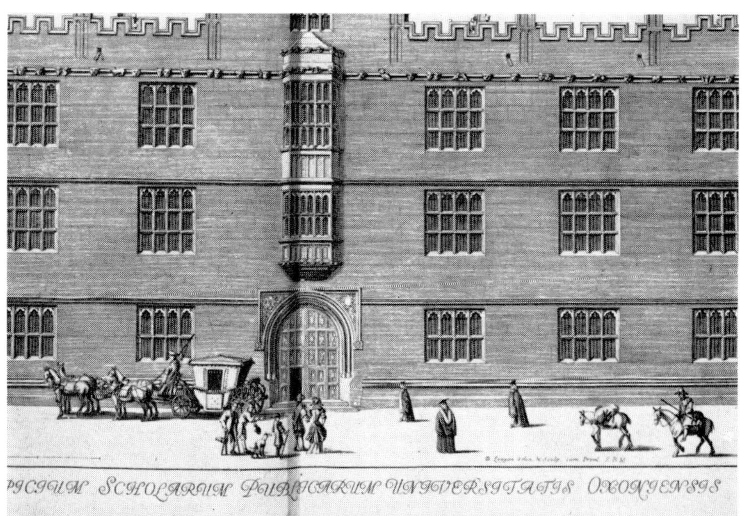

7 & 8. Coaches and packhorse traffic in Oxford, from D. Loggan's *Oxonia Illustrata* 1675

9. Title page of *A Post with a Paquet of Letters* 1633, by Nicholas Breton
10. *Courier Anglois*. A caricature by J. Bunbury 1774
(See Notes 027, 028)

NOTES

01

Carp by Waggon

Bishop Nicholson, who watched the netting of ponds at Brettenham in 1703, noted that twelve score carp that would have sold for £80 in former times were now 'not worth above £30'. He adds that 'the carp will carry alive to London in Straw or Grass, without water. Usually conveigh'd in Waggons; four Hoggsheads (of 80 fishes apiece) making a load'. (*Diaries*, Cumb. and West. Antiq. Society, N.S., I, 44.)

'It is a common practice in Holland to keep them alive for three weeks or a month by hanging them in a cool place with wet moss in a net, and feeding them with bread steeped in milk, taking care to refresh the animal now and then by throwing fresh water over the net in which it is suspended'. (*The Compleat Angler*, 1760, Ed. Hawkins.)

02

Carp pie

In 1653 Sir Ralph sent pies made from his own carp to friends in London. 'Mine', wrote Dr. Denton, 'was very good, but so full of small bones that none of us durst touch it, only to taste it'. Susan Abercromby, his widowed sister, now very poor, was at supper with them, and upon her praising it, the Doctor hastily presented her with the remains of the pie to take home with her. (*Memoirs of the Verney Family*, 1907, I, 535.)

03

Haulage by ox teams and horse teams

'If at any time on a farm where both oxen and horses were kept it happened that a horse team came to a standstill when hauling a thrashing machine, timber waggon, or any extra heavy load on a soft surface, they could always rely on the ox team to get them going again. The staunchest team of horses will try and try again, then they leap and dash at the collar, and if the load refuses to yield they chuck their heads up and give in.

'I have seen an ox team with such a job in hand, and their action is entirely different: they lean into the yoke, and if held they don't draw back, they only lean harder with every ounce of weight, every inch of muscle and sinew, and "Off she goes!" the teamster cries'. (W. Wood. *A Sussex Farmer*, 1938, p. 93.)

04

Unmetalled roads

'That soils, in general, if worn long enough, that is, deep enough would, on a gentle slope, afford a something to bear a horse or other animal may be true; for though a horse path may be poached in wet weather, yet in dry it is, in the nature of the tread of horses, trodden level again, to receive with benefit the water of heavy showers: but not one soil in a hundred is capable of affording materials sufficient to bear the wheels of laden carriages; which, in the action of wheel carriages, tend, not to fill up and level, but to deepen the holes and gutters made by running water; and of course act in concert with it to render the road impassable.' (W. Marshall. *Rural Economy of the Midland Counties*, 1796, I, 43.)

'A general method of raising roads in this and almost every other recluse District is to dig a deep ditch on either side; to cast the loose earth into the middle of the site; and on this to pile a narrow high ridge of hard materials. The effect is, carriages being necessarily confined to one track upon the ridge of the road, the stones which are not pressed into the loose dirt beneath are soon cut through by the wheels always passing in the same ruts, through which the artificial bog below soon rises to the surface. The method of repairing is equally absurd.

'Instead of the ruts being closed, by pecking in the ridges on either side of them, or by filling them with a few additional stones, the entire roadway is covered with a thick coat: and so often as fresh ruts are formed, so often is this expensive and therefore doubtly absurd method of repairing repeated: until having laid coat over coat, and piled ton upon ton unnecessarily, a mound of earth and stones, resembling the roof of a house rather than a road, is formed. . . .

'Upon the ridged up roads of this and other countries the driver of a top heavy load *dare* not leave the top of the ridge; and the drivers of loads which lie lower, for a variety of reasons, follow the beaten track: even horsemen who are timorous are afraid to leave it . . . no other part of the road being beaten, or convenient to travel upon.' (W. Marshall. *Rural Economy of Yorkshire*, 1788, I, 182, 186.)

05
Nails for shod carts

'Divers great nailes of iron were there found such as are used in the wheels of shod carts, being each of them as big as a man's finger, and a quarter of a yard long, the heads two inches over'. (Stow's *Survey of London*, 1598, Ed. Morley, p. 184.)

06

A young woman smothered

'Martha Warde, a young maid coming from Chelmsford on a carte, was overwhelmed and smothered with certain clothes which were in the carte, and was buried here. May 12. 1611'. (Parish Register of Saffron Walden quoted in *Old English Social Life*, 1898, by T. Thistleton Dyer, p. 169.)

07

Charged as half a pack

In 1582 carriage of a woolpack from Oswestry to London (120 miles) was 9*s*. Half a pack would therefore be 4*s*. 6*d*. But in 1573 the Nottingham carrier was paid 10*s*. 'for a hors for Elizabethe from London to Wolltaton (122) and for her charges'. (Tawney and Power *Economic Documents*, I, 201; *H.M. Com. Middleton*, p. 400.)

The carrier in *Long Meg of Westminster* 1582 demands 10*s*. for bringing her up from Lancashire, and is beaten for his presumption. But Long Meg would probably have resisted any demand. A curious point about this carrier is that in the early editions of the pamphlet he is a waggoner, but in the 1635 edition has become a packman. Somebody must have pointed out that a real Lancashire carrier would use pack-horses.

08

Country girls at Smithfield

'We hear of two or three new wenches are come up with a carrier, and your old goshawk here is flying at them' . . . 'How many carries hast thou bribed for country wenches?' (*The Honest Whore*, Pt. 2, III, 3, V2.)

W. C. Hazlitt in his *Fairy Mythology of Shakespeare* quotes the following:

When Virtue was a country maid
And had no skill to set up trade

She came up with a carrier's jade
  And lay at racke and manger;
She whift her pipe, she dranke her can,
The pot was ne're out of her span,
She married a tobacco man,
  A stranger, a stranger.

'On the King's being in Oxford, severall came downe to the Court, amongst which was one Mistress Kirk, daughter to one Mistress Townsend; she came to towne, as Mr Flexon, my barber, told mee, in a waggon, and in mean attire; hee saw her, for his Father kept the Chequers, where she lay. My Lord Lovelace took a lodging for her in All Soules, and after a while shee appeared as well clad as anie ladie in the Court.' (*Diary of the Rev. John Ward*, p. 143.)

09

Footmen and their drying money

'Item the xxiiij day of Decembre to Thomas Barton and Richard Chollerton the Quenes fotemen for thaire dryeng money, journeying with the Quenes said grace for a yere ended at Cristmas last past xij^{s} iiij^{d} (1502)'. (*Privy Purse Expenses of Elizabeth of York*, ed. Nichol.)

'Item paid to Jhon Hoggarde for wasshing hys hosse 6 nyght runyng a foote with my Lorde Rosse from th'Egle to London 6d; for a payr of shoys bought at Ware 12d; for 4 meales borde wages when he came to London 16d; for fyer in hys chamber the night that he came to London 4d . . . 3/2 (1550)'. (*H.M. Com. Rutland*, IV, 437.)

010

Footmen's uniform

It was the fashion to put these footmen into very elaborate uniform. 'They are turned out of their old habits into jackets of good preterpluperfect velvet, plated with silver, or *Argentum vivum* for the quickness, and all to be embroidered back and side with the best gold twist and the best of the silk worm . . . with such a deal of feather, ribbons and points, that he seems to be a running haberdasher's shop of small wares'. (John Taylor. *A Navy of Land Ships*, 1627.)

011

Cost of a postboy

Robert Loder estimates the yearly cost of a farm horse in 1612 at five pounds for feed, 13/4 for depreciation and 17/6 for shoeing and harness repairs.

His farm hands cost him about five pounds each in board, apart from wages.

A postboy's pay would probably consist of the groats that he earned as guide. In a busy week he might make the wage of a gentleman's groom. In the Bristol archives (*Mayor's Audits*) the wage of a groom is regularly entered as 4d a day in Henry VIII's reign, and as 6d a day in Elizabeth's.

012

Whirlicotes

The derivation and meaning of this word is uncertain. Perhaps a corruption of 'whurry-cart': a compound like 'go-cart', but based on the older form of the word 'hurry'. It is used in J. Weever' *Mirror of Martyrs*, 1601:

> Two fyrie coursers, foming clottred blood,
> Whurries, at last, Death bound in iron chaines; . . .

If this is correct, it would suggest that the whirlicote was a light, two wheeled vehicle (ancestor of the 'whiskey') and thus distinct from the 'chare' which had four wheels.

013

A Pomeranian coach, 1576

'*In primis* for sending one man into the country of Pomerland by my said lordes appoyntment to provide a strong cowche with all maner of furniture therto belonging and covered with leather, and viij wheles for the same cowche: which cowche being made with furniture for iiij horses: and also one manne to attend and govern the same: with the charges of conveing the same to London: cost £XLII.

'*Item* the same cowche was att Smithfield in London uncovered and made higher, the doing therof cost £VIII. 10s.'

(Account of the Steward of the Stillyard for procuring a coach for Sir Henry Sidney. *H.M. Com. de L'Isle and Dudley*, I, 265.)

014

Tall hats

'I pray, what were our Sugar loafe Hats, so mightily affected of late by men and women, so incommodious to use that every puffe of wind deprived us of them, requiring the employment of one hand to keep them on? Was it not the same conceit that the *Macrones* of *Pontus* and the *Macrocephali* once had, among whom they were esteemed the best Gentlemen who had the highest head? So our Gallants then to be different from the Vulgar heard, chose for a token of their Nobility to have sugar-loaf-like Hats; inso much as he was he was no Gentleman then that had not such a Hat'. (R. Bulwer. *Anthropometamorphosis*, 1650.)

015

Noblemen's coaches on hire

The coachman hired by Thomas Platter in 1599 excused himself from driving from Oxford to Cambridge by saying 'that the Coach was very expensive and belonged to a great Lord from whom he had hired it, and that he had newly set up house, and should the coach get stuck in the mud, he would be a broken man for life'. (*Thomas Platter's Travel in England*, ed. C. Williams, p. 217.)

016

Caroches

A bill for repair of the King's coaches 1625 mentions two new caroches, one of the Spanish fashion, and one of the German fashion 'with the roof to fall asunder at his Majesty's pleasure. . . . The like of them were never made before in England'. (*H.M. Com. 6th Report*, Appendix 327.)

017

The Spanish Ambassador's hat, 1612

'The Ambassador, Don Pedro de Zuniga, is yet here, no man knows why, for he hath taken his leave of the King. But to show that he is unwelcome, as he was riding in his carrosse with his six mules over Holborn Bridge the other day, with his great lechuguilla about his neck and coming upon his elbow, at the side of the carrosse comes a fellow by him on horseback; and whether de guet apens or otherwise I cannot tell, but he snatches the Ambassador's hat off his head, which had a rich jewel in it, and rides away with it up the street as fast as he could, the people going on and laughing at it.

'The fellow was not lighted on again, for anything I hear; but I am sorry they have so just an advantage against us to say we are barbarous in our city of London.' (T. Birch. *King James*, 1747, I, 191.)

018

Weight of coach wheels

In the Naworth Accounts (p. 342) the charge for carriage by pack from Newcastle seems to have varied between 2*s*. 3*d*. and 2*s*. 6*d*. per cwt. The charge for the two forewheels was 4*s*. 10*d*., and for the two hind wheels 'with other things' 9*s*. 10*d*.

019

Padded wheels

That the wheels of a town caroche were sometimes padded is suggested by the description of the Queen's chariot in Drayton's *Nimphidia* (1627):

'For fear of rattling on the stones
With Thistle down they shod it'.

Something of the kind was certainly needed. The chief streets in London were pitched with stones, which had sometimes been displaced by the traffic, leaving deep potholes. Dr. George Clarke remembered tumbling out of a coach when he was a child, just opposite the Horse Guards in Whitehall about 1665. 'My legs fell into a hole in the pavement, so that I received no prejudice on them by the coach wheels, which went pretty fast over them, but I had a great wound in my forehead'. (*H.M. Com. Leyborne Popham*, p. 259.)

020

The right Boot of a coach

'To be a Gentlewoman is a harder matter than you imagine; and 'tis not enough to take the Fan in hand, to clap the Patches on, and Paint too for a need, to be proud and disdaynful, and be coacht about, whilst you strive as much for the right Boote as others would do for their Birth right.' (Richard Flecknoe. *Heroick Portraits*, 1660, 'The portrait of Lysette, my Ladies half Gentlewoman'.)

021

Glass coaches

'The first glasse coach that came into England was the Duke of Yorke's when the King was restored. In a very short time they grew common, and now (1681) at Waltham, or Tottnam high crosse, is sett up a mill for grinding of coach glasses and looking glasses much cheaper'. (Aubrey. *Short Lives*, ed. Clark, II, 323.)

Robert Molesworth's new coach in 1706 was to have 'double chassis for canvas window in travelling as well as glass'. (*H.M. Com. Clements*, p. 34.)

022

Sussex roads

'The Sussex ways are bad and ruinous beyond imagination. I vow 'tis melancholy consideration that mankind will inhabit such a heap of dirt for a poor livelihood'. (Lord Chancellor Cowper, 1690, quoted by Wilson Hyde. *The Royal Mail*, 885, p. 4.)

023

Lob Lane

Commemorated in Aubrey's life of Bishop Corbet. 'His conversation was extreme pleasant. Dr. Stubbins was one of his Cronies; he was a jolly fatt Dr. and a very good Housekeeper; parson in Oxfordshire. As Dr. Corbet and he were riding in Lob Lane in wett weather ('tis an extraordinary deepe, dirty lane) the Coach fell; and Dr. Corbet sayd that Dr. Stubbins was up to the Elbowes in mud, he was up to the Elbowes in Stubbins'. (Aubrey. *Scandal and Credulities*, ed. Collier, 1931, p. 70.)

024

Trotting pack-horses

A trotting pack-train could sound like a troop of cavalry.

'Royalist troops under Captain Waithen marching from Hereford to Monmouth 1643 were ascending Llantawdy Hill when a trampling and clattering was heard as of armed horsemen coming down upon them through the hollow road. Panic struck they halted, and their commander himself . . . called out to those who were nearest, "If I fall, search my pockets"; . . . When lo! it was no more than a peaceful gang of carriers' horses hastening to the woods for charcoal; the rattling of whose trappings on their packsaddles had been the cause of such dismay'. (A tradition of the Wathen family narrated by J. Webb. *Memorials of the Civil War in Herefordshire*, I, 252.)

The metallic jingling was probably made by the 'wanty hooks': large metal hooks with 'safe' points to which the load was corded.

025

Lieutenant Dodington to the Counsell, July 25, 1599 (*Plate 1*)

(SP12/271.115. By permission of the Controller of H.M. Stationery Office)

Right Ho[ls] theire is a ffleet at this present bearinge in upon us, the wind at north west, by all likelyhode it should be the enymy. Hast makes me to think I can writ no more, I beseech yo Lo: to pardon me and so I refer all to yr Lo: most clocyst considerations.

Yo[r] Ho: most holly to
command
Ed Dodington

From the Work at Plymouth
the 25 of Julie 1599

It was a false alarm; but it rattled the Lieutenant and deranged the spelling and routine of his orderly clerk. He ought to have used a "label" or "scroll" for a packet like this, (p. 75), but this was no time for decorums. He folded the letter twice into an oblong three leaves thick, turned the ends back so as to meet with a small overlap, fixed them with a gout of wax, scrawled a rather drunken looking gallows on the front, and marked it emphatically for Her Majesty's "Cervise", (*cervisia* being the Latin for strong ale). He was not responsible for the crease across the middle of the letter, which must have been made later by some filing clerk.

The endorsements at the post stages were made chiefly on the back of the packet wherever there happened to be room, Deciphered and put in order they give the following record of this letter's progress:

Plymouth		7 pm	
Ashburton	27	2 am	4 mph
Exeter	19	6	5
Honiton	17	8	8
Crewkerne	21	11	7
Sherborne	14	1 pm	7
Shaftesbury	15	4	5
Salisbury	20		
Andover	18	8 am	2·3
Basingstoke	19	1 pm	4
Hartford Bdge	10	3.30	4
Staines	19	7 (?)	5½

The first two stages out of Plymouth were ridden at night which accounts for the moderate speed. The post could not gallop down lanes like Dean Clapperhill even on the cleverest moor pony. With Thursday's daylight the pace mended: 8 mph to Honiton, 7 to Crewkerne, and 7 to Sherborne. The road near Crewkerne must have been pestered with traffic returning from Chard Fair (July 25) but the postboy managed to keep up the speed prescribed for summer riding. At

Sherborne it was market day and dinner time when the post rode in, which may account for the fall to 5 mph over the next stage. But after Shaftesbury something went seriously wrong. There is no record of the letter at Salisbury, and when next seen it is moving slowly into Andover at 8 am on Friday morning; having travelled the 38 miles of good road from Shaftesbury at little more than two miles an hour, a disgraceful performance. But we happen to know that the post of Salisbury, John Dowley, was unsatisfactory. The Mayor had complained to Lord Stanhope in the previous year that people had reported meeting "a boy of the said Dowley three miles from Salisbury . . . riding towards Shaftesbury with important letters, and his horse was so tired that the boy was forced to walk." (H.M. Com. *Cecil*, VIII, 233.) Dowley may still have been using this insufficient horse for night riding in which high speed could not be demanded. After Andover the pace picked up a little; but all sense of urgency had gone out of the business on Salisbury Plain. If the time of receipt at Staines was 7 pm, the letter had taken 48 hours to travel the 193 miles from Plymouth.

Dowley probably ought to have been dismissed. But the post of a provincial town was not easy to replace. His monopoly had probably given him the town's largest livery stable, to which everyone came for horses in an emergency. It would be very difficult for his successor in the postship to carry out the duties without his good will. He was thus in a position to do as he liked, and John Dowley was still post of Salisbury in 1602.

026

Riding Boots of a Postboy 1650 (*Plate 2*)

These boots cost about 8/- a pair, and were worn with thick baize 'vamps', or stockings, which could be made out of an old table cloth. (*The Life of Sir George Radcliffe* ed. Whitaker, 1810 p. 65.) It was difficult to walk and impossible to run in them. Some of Wyatt's adherents, hotly pursued after their defeat at Wrotham, "were driven to leave their horse, and creepe into the woode, and for haste to rippe their bootes from theyr legges, and runne awaye in the vampage of their hose". (Grose. *Antiquarian Repository*. 1809, 111, 82.)

027

Detail from the title page of *A Post with a Paquet of Letters*, 1633 by Nicholas Breton. (*Plate 9*)

The seventeenth century woodcuts represent the postboy or man as more smartly dressed and better horsed than he usually was. His horn was an ordinary hunting horn, and its sound was not distinctive. It was therefore easy for a sportsman to clear the road for himself by imitating the post. The draft Regulations of 1575 make it an offence "for anie other man that weareth a horne, to blow his horne in the highe waye to cause other to geve place, as manie have used to doe for their pleasure".

The bag at this early period was a satchel slung over the shoulder of the postboy. But under the system adopted by Witherings in 1635 the bags of letters for the towns on a high road were all packed in a "portmantle", and carried on an additional horse. The portmantles were indistinguishable from a passenger's luggage, and were sometimes forwarded on the horse of the guide hired by a private traveller.

028

Courier Anglois (*Plate 10*)

A caricature by J. Bunbury 1774. No doubt exaggerated, but it illustrates how the growth of correspondence had turned the postboy's bag into an enormous sack, and his horse into an ordinary pack horse upon which he travels in the old carriers' fashion as "half the pack". There is no appearance of haste, but he is blowing an impressive looking coach horn. The time was ripe for Mr John Palmer's Mail Coaches (1784).

Index